Sisters

Mary Magdalene and the Women in Jesus' Life

Joseph and Carolyn Grassi

Sheed & Ward

Copyright © 1986
Joseph and Carolyn Grassi

Sheed and Ward™ is a service of National Catholic Reporter Publishing, Inc.

Library of Congress Catalog Card Number: 85-63575

ISBN: 0-934134-33-2

Published by:

Sheed & Ward
115 E. Armour Blvd. P.O. Box 414292
Kansas City, MO 64141-0281

To order, call: 800-821-7926

Contents

INTRODUCTION

Was the relationship between Jesus and Mary Magdalene a matter of fact, fiction, or fantasy? Was Mary a woman disciple, a friend, or a spouse of Jesus? Or all three? This book responds to these questions through a study of the life and mission of Jesus as seen from the viewpoint of a woman in first century Israel. Reading between the lines of the New Testament we uncover the embarrassing truth (for ancient times) that women played an essential role in the life of Jesus and the origins of Christianity. Jesus' teaching envisioned a peace movement and a non-violent life style in face of the acute political and social oppression of his country. This was especially appreciated and understood within the inner and personal world of women and children.

After Jesus' death, Mary Magdalene's name and importance continued on within the secret teachings and documents of gnostic Christians. They saw her as a model for the true believer — one who wished to enter into a deep spiritual union with Christ. This book will especially interest the reader who desires to investigate the feminine element in Jesus' teachings, relationships and in the early church. It will also be important for anyone today who wishes to explore the implications of "God made them male and female" for the interrelationship of man and woman in modern society.

We should make the following note on history for our readers:

The four gospels were not interested in newspaper-type reporting. They were interested in history but in a very special sense. They were especially concerned to provide us with the *meaning* of Jesus' life in view of a mysterious plan of God which they found in their ancient Scriptures, in what Christians call the Old Testament. Consequently, they often selected only those facts and details about Jesus' life which they felt were most useful to illustrate how he fulfilled this plan of God. They skipped over many things that did not have any correspondence with the Old Testament Scriptures.

Our purpose in writing is similar: to uncover the meaning of Jesus' life and mission especially in regard to Mary Magdalene and the other women in his life. Sometimes we will rely on creative imagination for details in order to bring out this meaning. However, at all times we will try to do so in accord with the information modern biblical study has given us on the New Testament and the historical, political, economic and social situation in Israel in the first century.

**Note: The abbreviation *NHL* indicates the *Nag Hammadi Library*.

1. MARY MAGDALENE, THE WOMAN IN JESUS' LIFE

Fact, Fiction or Fantasy?

For most people the first image of Mary of Magdala is that of the flamboyant courtesan of Galilee, sought after ardently by countless men — the woman who goes through a dramatic conversion and throws herself at Jesus' feet, washing them with her tears and drying them with her hair. Or the vivid picture of her singing "I don't know how to love him," from *Jesus Christ Superstar* with all the glamour and pathos that Broadway and Hollywood can exploit on the stage or screen.

Yet a question disturbs our images and fantasies: Just how much of this portrayal is authentic? Is there any evidence that she was Jesus' best friend, *the* woman in his life? Or have a few insignificant details about her been exaggerated to the heights of absurdity? What is the real story behind Jesus and this Mary that we obtain from authentic sources? By authentic sources we mean the four gospels, Matthew, Mark, Luke and John, along with those documents close enough to the time of the gospels' composition to give us reliable information.

1

How Important Is She?

The central message of the gospels, and indeed of Christianity, is that Jesus died, was buried and rose from the dead. Without this, the four gospels crumble and fall, becoming a collection of pointless tales from the distant past. Without these central events, Christianity loses its credibility and becomes a great deception. Yet the most important among the few witnesses of these three events is Mary Magdalene. Just after the death of Jesus, the gospel of Mark, perhaps the earliest witness, notes the following (after noting that an unknown Roman centurion witnessed his death):

> There were also women looking on from afar, among
> whom were Mary Magdalene and Mary the mother
> of James the younger of Joseph, and Salome . .
> .(15:40).

The gospel of Matthew has the same list. Only the gospel of John has the mother of Jesus, as well as her sister near the cross, for reasons we shall see later.

When it comes to the burial of Jesus, the list narrows down:

> Mary Magdalene and Mary the mother of Joseph saw
> where he was laid (Mark 15:47). Mary Magdalene
> and the other Mary were there, sitting opposite the
> sepulcher (Matthew 27:61).

It can be noted that Mary, the mother of Joseph or "the other Mary," does not seem to be very important. She is not mentioned elsewhere, and may simply be a companion to Mary Magdalene, who is the first and most important. The only other burial witness is Joseph of Arimathea, to whom the gospel of John adds Nicodemus.

Likewise, Mary Magdalene is the key person among the witnesses to Jesus' empty tomb and his resurrection. In Mark's gospel, the women came early Sunday morning to Jesus' tomb to anoint his body. This is because Jesus died shortly before sunset on Friday, when the Sabbath began. During the Sabbath, they were not able to buy and prepare the necessary spices to anoint his body.

> And when the sabbath was past, Mary Magdalene, and Mary the mother of James, and Salome, bought spices, so that they might go and anoint him. And very early on the first day of the week they went to the tomb when the sun had risen (Mark 16:1-2).

Matthew does not mention the anointing, and simply says that Mary Magdalene and "the other Mary" went to *see* the sepulcher (28:1). Luke mentions the same two women and adds the name of Joanna (24:10). In the gospel of John, it is *only* Mary Magdalene who comes to the tomb on Easter morning, and she is the first to notice that the tomb is empty (20:1-2).

In regard to the resurrection of Jesus: in Mark's gospel, Mary and her companions are the *only* ones who enter the tomb and see a young man (an angel?) dressed in a white robe who announces to them,

> Do not be amazed; you seek Jesus of Nazareth, who was crucified. He has risen, he is not here (16:6).

The women are then told to bring this message to Peter and the disciples:

> Go, tell his disciples and Peter that he is going before you to Galilee; there you will see him, as he told you.

The gospel of Mark ends with the women running from the tomb in a state of shock and astonishment. (The verses that follow [9-19] are commonly considered a later addition to the gospel.)

Mark's account prompts us to conclude that the testimony of Mary Magdalene and her companions is crucial for the beginnings of Christianity. In the gospel of John, Mary Magdalene (alone) is the first to have a vision of the Risen Christ after his death. She also hastens to tell the other disciples what she has seen (John 20:14-18). In the gospel of Matthew, the first appearance of Jesus is to Mary Magdalene along with her companion, "the other Mary" (28:1; 28:9-10).

Again we ask: how much actual history lies behind the gospel accounts? There is no doubt the gospels are "biased." They are confessional documents written by believers for believers. Yet in all ancient documents there is one criterion that almost infallibly points to the truth: If a document mentions matters that cause serious difficulty or embarrassment to the author, it is very probable he/she would omit it unless it were a very important fact. In the ancient world, the fact that Christianity owed its beginnings to the witness of one or two women would be a very difficult message to proclaim. This is not only due to women's status in the ancient world, but because in the Jewish world of Jesus' time, the witness of women was not admitted in any law case or civil procedure.

It was indeed very embarrassing for the early church to face the fact that all Jesus' male disciples quickly ran off when Jesus was arrested. Matthew simply notes: "Then all the disciples abandoned him and fled" (26:56; see also Mark 14:50). The twelve were afraid they might be considered fellow revolutionaries and supporters of Jesus. Thus only women are left as witnesses of the crucial events of Jesus' life: his death, burial and resurrection. We can see why Luke omits the description of the flight of Jesus' male disciples. He also seems to be very concerned about the mention of only women as witnesses to the death of Christ that he finds in Mark, one of his sources. Consequently, he adds other witnesses alongside the women in a cryptic expression, "All his acquaintances" (23:49).

Mary Magdalene was not a brief acquaintance of Jesus, but

a longtime associate. She had previously been in Galilee with him, and accompanied him on his last journey to Jerusalem. Mark writes (about Mary Magdalene, the other Mary, and Salome):

> These (women) when he was in Galilee, followed him and ministered to him: and also many other women who came up with him to Jerusalem (15:40).

Later we shall see more in detail what it meant to be a follower of Jesus, and to "minister" to him. For now it is enough to note that to be a follower of Jesus meant to be in his company and imitate his life-style. To "minister" to him would be to take care of his personal needs such as food, clothing, etc.

Mary Magdalene's presence at the crucifixion of Jesus and her careful notice of how and where he was buried, along with her visit to his burial spot, involved extreme risk. It meant immediate identification as one of Jesus' followers — an accomplice of the crucified revolutionary in Roman eyes. Peter and the Twelve were not willing to take this risk and fled from the Master at his arrest. Mary Magdalene's action involved heroic devotion. What greater love could there be? Even Jesus had said, "Greater love has no person than this, that a person lay down his/her life for a friend" (John 15:13).

Being a disciple of Jesus meant involvement in a close knit community, which Jesus considered more important to him than natural family ties. On one occasion, when his mother and family were outside a home filled with his disciples, and they sent for him to come out, Jesus looked at his disciples around him and said,

> "Who are my mother and brothers?" And looking around on those who sat about him, he said, "Here are my mother and my brothers. Whoever does the will of God is my brother, and sister, and mother." (Mark 3:31-35)

Mary Magdalene, and other women like her, were esteemed as sisters in Jesus' own family. They were even called "sister," a custom followed by the early Christian church.

Looking now from Jesus' standpoint, Mary Magdalene was not only a close disciple, but also a woman who ministered to his personal needs as well as being a "sister" in his close-knit family of disciples. However, there appears to be much more. She is always named first by Matthew, Mark and Luke among the women disciples of Jesus. (cf. the texts quoted earlier.) Also, in the view of the early Christian church, the resurrection appearances of Jesus were not due to merely subjective experience. It is quite evident that Jesus chose Mary as the first to whom he appeared, according to John and the first among the women who saw him according to Matthew and Luke. The longer ending of Mark also has this,

> Now when he rose early on the first day of the week,
> he appeared first to Mary Magdalene, from whom
> he had cast out seven demons (16:9).

The traditional importance of Mary Magdalene and her closeness to Jesus was emphasized in early Christianity also. In Chapter 13, we examine closely the connection between Mary Magdalene and the lost Christians, as found in the recently discovered gnostic gospels and documents. In these sources, she is considered the source of a secret revelation from Jesus that is very important to these Christians. For the moment, we can note here some of the texts that underline Mary's closeness to Jesus. The *Gospel of Philip* has these statements,

> There were three who always walked with the Lord:
> Mary, his mother, and her sister and the Magdalene,
> the one who was called a companion. His mother and
> her sister and his companion were each a Mary (*NHL*
> II, 3:59, 8-10).

Also,

> . . . the companion of the Savior was Mary Mag-
> dalene. (But Christ loved) her more than (all) the
> disciples (and used to) kiss her (often) on her (mouth).
> The rest of (the disciples were offended) by it (and
> expressed disapproval). They said to him, "Why do
> you love her more than all of us?" (*NHL* II, 3:63,
> 34-64, 5)

The kiss was a common sign of greeting, and in the gospel
of Philip it has a special meaning, which we refer to in Chapter
12.

The Gospel of Mary is centered about Mary Magdalene and
the special revelation she has received from Jesus. In it Peter
says to her,

> We know that the Savior loved you more than the
> rest of women. Tell us the words of the Savior which
> you remember (*NHL, BG* 10, 4-5).

From all this we can only conclude that Jesus and Mary
Magdalene were *most* important to each other. Yet just what
was their relationship? Was it favorite disciple, associate, friend
or even spouse? To even begin to answer these questions we
must explore the first important decision points of Jesus' life:
his meeting with the fiery John the Baptist, his baptismal experience itself, and his public announcement of the imminent
coming of the kingdom of God. These events would eventually
affect all his human relationships, especially with women.

2. THE CARPENTER FROM NAZARETH

Jesus, as a young man, had a comfortable career ahead of him. No one could have guessed that in a few years he would end up on the cross apparently executed as a dangerous revolutionary. To label Jesus as a "poor carpenter" is to misunderstand his profession. A carpenter could be called the local building contractor in those days. He built the homes, the bridges, the public buildings of the day. If there were such a group, Jesus could be called a member of the "upper middle class." When he became poor on beginning his mission, it was a voluntary poverty by choice not a necessary condition of life. When he asked his disciples to sell what they had and share with poor, he was only asking them to do what he had already done in a voluntary manner.

As Jesus walked through the narrow streets of his home town, did he carry an uneasiness in his heart despite his own material well-being? Was he not struck by the extremes of riches and poverty that met his eyes? There were rows of dilapidated shacks from which hungry, ill-clad children ran in and out to play in the streets. As he walked along, he was probably interrupted by beggars, some blind, some disabled. They stopped his journey with their cries, until he could find a coin to assist them.

From the top of the hill of Nazareth, Jesus would be able to see below him the rich farming land of the plain of Genezareth. Part of it was divided into small plots, from which individual families could eke out a meager existence. The rest was owned by rich landlords who maintained beautiful homes in the city. They worked their land either by paying day-laborers a pitiful wage or by renting it out to tenants and sharecroppers.

Jesus lived in a land of injustice. What was the cause of this injustice? Anyone, whether a child on the street, a woman at a well, or a merchant at his stand would say the cause was Rome! Almost two generations had passed since Roman legions under Pompey in 63 B.C. had taken away their land and independence. Now they were economic slaves and serfs of the mightiest empire the world had ever known. Rome had no philosophy of assisting "developing countries." The far-flung provinces were considered rich prizes for the increasing greed of the capital city. They were also coveted political plums given to faithful political or military leaders who could be awarded a governorship as an opportunity to amass an abundant "retirement fund."

The Roman system of taxation was carefully organized all over the world. There was a fourfold tax: first a land tax payable either in produce or money; secondly, there was a graduated income tax; thirdly, a poll tax for every single person except children or the aged; finally there were custom duties on all imports and exports from each Roman province. The tax burden was made even heavier by the fact that the office of tax collector was farmed out to the highest bidders who were notorious for their ability to overcharge the people in order to get a good return on their investment. Failure to pay meant prison or severe punishment at the hands of the Roman military.

The region of Galilee bore a double burden of oppression. Not

only Rome pressed deeply into every pocket. There was Herod
also, the Jewish puppet king whom Rome allowed to govern
this region in her name. Herod brought to the court of his tiny
kingdom the luxury and splendor he had observed in large
nations, even what he had seen in Rome itself. Herod was not
content to maintain a luxurious palace in Galilee. The cool
winter winds coming down from the snow-covered slopes of
Mount Hermon were too much for the pleasure-loving monarch.
He also kept a winter palace on a warm spot overlooking the
Dead Sea. This palace was an almost impregnable citadel that
was later used by Zealot revolutionaries to make a final, bitter
stand against Rome after the fall of Jerusalem in 70 A.D. This
final stand is immortalized in the story of Masada.

As Jesus looked over the valley from his Nazareth hill top,
the clouds themselves seemed to be part of a hot, oppressive,
heavy blanket covering the whole valley. Jesus' heart also became heavy and his muscles ached. But just then a cool breeze
sprang up. His sadness faded away and his face began to smile.
He was reminded that conditions in his beloved land could
change just as quickly as a summer breeze cools the landscape.
Beneath the sorrows and burden of Jesus and his people, there
was an irrepressible hope and confidence that a great change
could take place almost at any moment.

This hope was based on the very nature of their mysterious
God YHWH, whose name was so sacred and holy the Jews did
not dare pronounce it. The word *Adonai* or LORD was usually
substituted for it. It was this God who had revealed his name
to Moses in a burning bush near Sinai some thirteen centuries
before (Exodus 3:1-15). This YHWH had revealed himself as a
powerful God of history. He was a liberating God, who chose
to be with his people to free them from all external bondage.
He had freed them (around 1300 B.C.) by mighty signs when
they were slaves of Egypt, the most powerful nation of the
world at that time. In giving them the Ten Commandments on
Mount Sinai he declared,

> I am the LORD your God who brought you out of the
> land of Egypt, out of the house of bondage (Exodus
> 20:1-2).

Adonai was often called a God of hosts (heavenly armies)
because he had repeatedly shown his power in history in the
face of impossible odds. After the temple had been destroyed
by the Babylonian world rulers in 587 B.C., it was YHWH, who
led the Persians to overthrow Babylon and allowed them to
return home from exile in Babylon to rebuild their temple and
their country.

Yet the most dramatic intervention of YHWH had occurred
not in the distant past, but under their Greek rulers in 164
B.C. Alexander the Great, around 333 B.C., had conquered the
Persians and brought his control and power even as far as India
in the east. After his untimely death, the Greek world was
divided into three parts among Alexander's generals, who estab-
lished three dynasties. The Greeks considered themselves not
just as conquerors but as "missionaries." They had achieved a
remarkably high level of culture and felt it their duty to "en-
lighten" the world by teaching the Greek language, sciences
and system of education.

The Greeks promoted this plan for the "Hellenization" of the
world mainly by governmental pressures of persuasion, estab-
lishing Greek schools throughout the empire. We owe our word
gymnasium to the Greek school system. *Gymnos* means naked.
Many of the physical exercises in the all-male school were performed naked. To physical training was united training in the
arts, music and grammar as well as training in the virtues. It
was the Greek model of "holistic" education.

The Greek program of "modernization" was vigorously pur-
sued among the Jews also. The Jewish book of the Maccabees
tells us that Antiochus Epiphanes came into power around 175
B.C. and made a renewed effort to Hellenize the Jews. The
results were at first impressive. Many "progressive" Jews

adopted Greek ways, abandoning centuries of religious tradition. The author of 1 Maccabees sadly writes,

> So they (the Hellenized Jews) built a gymnasium in
> Jerusalem, according to Gentile custom, and re-
> moved the marks of circumcision, and abandoned
> the holy covenant. They joined with the Gentiles and
> sold themselves to do evil (1:15-16).

This "removal of circumcision" was a painful surgical operation to cover their circumcision, which was the visible sign (so
evident in the gymnasium!) that they were Jews, obliged to
keep all the commandments of their Law.

However, the Hellenization progress was not quick enough
for Antiochus. He finally issued an edict that forbade Jews from
observing the Sabbath; women who had their babies circum-
cised were ordered to be executed with their babies around
their necks; scrolls of the Law and Bible were publicly burned;
finally the temple itself was desecrated and closed so sacrifices
could no longer be offered (1 Maccabees 1:45-75).

Israel had reached the lowest ebb in her history. Their mighty
God YHWH appeared to be a helpless victim of the proud Greek
ruler who even proclaimed himself a god — Antiochus
"Epiphanes" (god-manifest) and placed his image in public
places to be venerated.

There was, however, one family, that of Mattathias which
refused to go along with the king's edict. They withdrew into
the wilderness, where other fervent supporters of the Law and
Jewish tradition joined them. At first they seemed no match
for the trained, better equipped and vastly outnumbering forces
of King Antiochus. However, the Jewish freedom fighters had
a secret weapon that no one could withstand, no matter what
odds were in their favor. This secret weapon was their absolute
and almost fanatic confidence that YHWH was fighting their

battles for them and that they were certain of victory. As a result, after long and bitter fighting, the Greek forces were defeated and the temple was rededicated around 164 B.C.

This great victory is still commemorated by Jews all over the world in the feast of *Hannukah* or Dedication, celebrated for seven days during December. After this, from 164-63 B.C. the Jews enjoyed once again a period of freedom and independence — until the Romans came. In the mind of Jesus and his contemporaries, God's victory over the Greeks was an infallible sign of what would happen to the Romans also. It was only a matter of time.

Jesus and his fellow Jews prayed: "How long, O Lord, before deliverance?" They believed that God's plan was behind human events and eventually the liberation of Israel would take place. At times, privileged individuals, after long prayer and fasting, had been able to obtain a glimpse of the divine plans through visions and then reveal them to the people.

This is why the mysterious book of Daniel was the cherished book of every Jew. Here the Jews were told how the prophet Daniel, through dreams and revelation came to know the divine timetable for history and predict the restoration of the temple, the defeat of the Greeks, and the liberation of Israel. Daniel had discovered this divine timetable through finding a hidden meaning in the ancient Scriptures. In Chapter 9 of the prophet, the mysterious story was told. Daniel had been searching the Scriptures for light in regard to the terrible crisis of his time. He came upon the book of Jeremiah (25:11-12; 29:10) where the prophet had predicted that God would restore his people from the Babylonian exile (after 587 B.C.) at the end of 70 years.

Daniel stopped at this passage and prayed all day for inspiration, not even stopping to eat or drink so nothing would disturb his intense prayer. Toward evening, at the time of the temple evening sacrifice, he had a vision of the angel Gabriel coming to him to give the answer to his prayer: the seventy

weeks of years were God's historical plan. The final week was
the time of Antiochus' triumph. The last half-week was his
great victory in closing the temple to sacrifice. But all of this
was but a prelude to a great dramatic reversal when God himself would overturn the Greek king and establish his kingdom
once more (9:27).

Now during Jesus' time under the Romans, history was repeating itself. The divine timetable was moving along steadily.
The time seemed ripe for the heavens to burst open. Somehow
Jesus had the inner feeling that the chosen messenger to reveal
God's plan was indeed alive; he had only to find him. But where
to look? A sudden thought crossed Jesus' mind: he must seek
out John the Baptist by the Jordan River.

We do not know what circumstances led Jesus to make the
long journey south to Judea and down to the Jordan River to
seek out John the Baptist. But we do know from the gospel of
John (1:35-50) that several disciples of the Baptist, at least
Andrew, Peter and Philip were there from Galilee. Perhaps
they had sent back news about a fiery preacher near the Jordan
who was announcing that the long expected Kingdom of God
was almost at hand. Such an announcement was just the spark
needed to flare up the smoldering fire of messianic expectation
that lay in everyone's heart. Crowds of people flocked to the
Jordan to hear the Baptist from Jerusalem, all Judea, and even
distant Galilee.

Here again, we must apply the tools of historical criticism.
How are we to understand the beginnings of Jesus' ministry
and the initial impulse that was to shape his whole mission?
Once again we apply the criterion: the mention of important
embarrassing events indicates they could not be left out without
jeopardizing the whole message. In this case, it was not easy
for the early church to emphasize the strong link between Jesus
and the Baptist; for Jesus came *to* him and was baptized *by*
him; some of Jesus' first disciples, notably Peter, Andrew and
Philip had been previously followers of the Baptist; Jesus' first

preaching, "the kingdom of God is at hand," was also that of John.

But why is the link embarrassing? Because John the Baptist was an important historical figure, mentioned outside the gospels by the Jewish historian Josephus. After Jesus' death, there were many disciples of the Baptist scattered over the world, some of whom had not become Christians (see Acts of the Apostles 18:24-25; 19:1-7). Naturally, Christians entered into discussions with them about who was the greatest or more important, Jesus or the Baptist? The adherents of the Baptist certainly emphasized that their founder came *first* and actually was the one who baptized Jesus.

It is very important for us, then, to study the relationship between John and Jesus and to see how the experience at the Jordan shaped Jesus' entire mission and life, especially his relationship to Mary Magdalene and other women.

3. THE FIERY BAPTIST BY THE JORDAN AND THE BAPTISM OF JESUS

Jesus began the long three-day walk from Galilee to the valley of the Jordan River near the Dead Sea where John was baptizing. A great decision in his life lay ahead of him. The final stage of his journey led him down to the lowest area of the earth, the Dead Sea, some 1200 feet below sea level. The earth's gravitational force made him feel his body weigh him down, step by step. But there was also an inner gravity that was pulling him deeper and deeper into a mystery he did not understand.

Even from a distance he could hear the roaring voice of the Baptist above the rushing waters of the Jordan. Again and again the Baptist cried out, "Repent, the Kingdom of God is at hand." As Jesus drew near, he was surprised by what he saw. There was an unkempt, bearded young man, clothed only with a garment of rough camel's hair, with a belt of skins around his waist. He was dressed exactly like the great prophet Elijah (2 Kings 1:8) who had come to warn Israel many centuries before. At that time, people had forgotten YHWH and turned to fertility worship. The Scriptures hinted that Elijah had not really died: YHWH himself came down in a chariot of fire to bring him to heaven (2 Kings 2:11). It was a common belief that Elijah would return before the great Day of the Lord when God would intervene on earth to rescue Israel from the oppressors. The last words of the last prophet in the Bible, Malachi, expressed this hope:

> Lo, I will send you Elijah the Prophet before the great and terrible day of the Lord comes and he will turn the hearts of fathers to their children and the hearts of children to their fathers (3:24).

Jesus knew that Malachi had emphasized a message of repentance, a turning of the heart, just like the Baptist. Could John be the great prophet, an Elijah returned, who was destined to announce a New Age for Israel and the world?

Something unusual was happening. John was standing with his feet in the Jordan River. People were coming up to him in a single file waiting for him to plunge their bodies under the water as a sign of total conversion and entry into the New Age. At first, Jesus was taken back when he witnessed this scene. Baptism or total immersion was reserved for Gentile pagans who wished to convert to Judaism. Such a sign indicated their desire to live new lives, and accept circumcision as well as the whole Jewish Law.

John was saying in effect that it was not enough to be a Jew to be part of the Kingdom of God. A total change of life, as dramatic as that of a pagan convert was necessary. Pharisees and Sadducees, some of whom were even priests, also approached John for baptism. Here were the Pharisees, perfect observers of the Law, and priests of the Holy Temple. No doubt they expected to be baptized immediately without any questions asked. But no, the stern Baptist turned them away with these words:

> You brood of vipers! Who warned you to flee from
> the wrath to come? Bear fruit that befits repentance,
> and do not presume to say to yourselves, "We have
> Abraham as our father." (Matthew 3:7-9)

These were hard words to hear, especially when they looked
around at the type of people John was welcoming with open
arms: despised tax collectors working for Rome; rough soldiers
and even women who had been prostitutes. They were people
who felt the need of God's forgiveness and mercy, unlike some
Jewish religious leaders who felt themselves already clean and
pure. Openly, the repentant sinners confessed their sins before
John, and were baptized. For each, John had specific words of
counsel about how their lives could be changed. To tax collectors
he said, "Collect no more than is appointed you" (Luke 3:13).
To soldiers, "Rob no one by violence or by false accusation, be
content with your wages." To many others he simply repeated,
"He who has two coats, let him share with him who has none,
and he who has food, let him do likewise" (3:11).

Jesus stood at the turning point of his life. He looked up to
heaven and prayed for guidance and strength. At once he knew
what he must do; there was no turning back. He took his place
in the line of humble sinners waiting for their turn for baptism.
When he came to John their eyes met, but there was also a
meeting that took place in their inner beings. Somehow they
both felt they were to be associated in a dramatic moment of
history. With hesitation and solemnity, John took Jesus' body
into his hands and plunged it into the flowing waters of the
Jordan.

When Jesus lifted his head from the water and dried the
water from his eyes, he felt a sudden gust of wind. He looked
up to the skies and was amazed by what he saw and heard.
The gospel of Mark tells the story simply,

> Immediately he saw the heavens opened and the

Spirit descending on him like a dove, and a voice
came from heaven, "You are my beloved Son; with
you I am well pleased." (1:11)

The whole vision was brief, perhaps only a matter of seconds,
yet Jesus was completely stunned. John the Baptist must have
realized that something very significant had happened to Jesus.
However, it is not likely that he observed the vision and heard
the words. Biblical revelations and visions are not public events,
but secrets perceived only by those to whom they are directed.

Jesus needed a time of silence, reflection and prayer to understand the implications of this profound vision for his whole life.
He immediately withdrew into the wild, uninhabited area above
the Jordan River. For forty days he remained there, neither
eating nor drinking while he prayed and pondered about what
might lie before him.

He knew very well that a voice from heaven meant that he
was designated for a very special mission. The words, "You are
my son" immediately recalled God's own words addressed to
the Pharaoh of Egypt through Moses when Israel was an oppressed people of slaves:

Thus says the LORD: Israel is my first born-son, and
I say to you, let my son go, that he may serve me
(Exodus 4:22).

With the words, "You are my son", Jesus felt a very strong
identification with the whole history and goals of his people
Israel. He was designated to bring them to completion as a
chosen leader or Messiah, the Anointed One. He was the long-
awaited instrument of God to bring liberation to the oppressed
of Israel.

At the same time the word *son* had a very strong meaning
of complete and dedicated obedience. Again and again it had
been used in the Scriptures with this meaning. Jesus knew

well the image of the perfect son that every Jew took as a model. This was Isaac in the story told in Genesis 22. God had commanded Abraham,

> Take your son, your only son Isaac whom you love,
> and go to the land of Moriah and offer him there as
> a burnt offering upon one of the mountains of which
> I shall tell you (22:2).

The word "beloved" or "whom you love" is the same word addressed to Jesus in the heavenly voice at his baptism. In the Genesis story Abraham promptly obeys despite what appears to be an impossible and even contradictory command. He was asked to sacrifice the very son whom God had promised him, the son who would give him a posterity numerous as "the sand on the seashore" or the "stars in the sky." Jewish piety stressed the obedience of Isaac, who, as a young man, was willing to go ahead and offer himself because he listened to the voice of God coming from his father Abraham. As the story turns out, God did not want the sacrifice of Isaac. An angel intervenes at the last moment. What God did wish was complete obedience, an obedience even as far as death. As Jesus reflected on the meaning of the voice from heaven, he knew that to be a real son of God and take up the destiny of his people meant the most perfect union of will between himself and God his Father, an obedience as far as death.

Jesus took a deep breath. He had been taught as a child (like other Jewish children) to be especially aware of his breathing. After his baptism a deeper feeling about the importance of this came to him. In the first book of the bible (Genesis) he had often heard the story of how God breathed into the first man and woman so that they became living beings (2:7). Jesus knew that the Scriptures were not meant to be books of the ancient past, but were written to tell him who he was here and now. It was the very breath of God, the source of all life that was in him, the divine element present in every man and woman. The Hebrew text called this the *Ruach* (the breath) or the *Ruach Haqodesh* the Holy Breath or Holy Spirit. It was this Holy Breath or Spirit that had first begun the whole process of the creation of the world (Genesis 1:2). It was present in every plant, animal and living being. The Jews thought of it in terms of energy, the divine energy that filled the whole universe. To give attention and awareness to one's breathing was to feel the power of this energy within every living creature. The bible even defines humanity as "all those in whose nostrils is the breath of life" (Genesis 7:22). God's Holy Breath was the source of all life and breath on earth.

But when Jesus experienced the Spirit coming upon him at his baptism, it was of much more profound depth and dimension. This Spirit now quickened him with a new fullness of divine energy, an abiding presence that guided and directed his life. It was something he could feel in the depths of his heart as an inner warmth and power that was beyond anything he had ever experienced before. Jesus spent many days and hours pondering over the new meaning this presence would have for him. In his search for enlightenment, he recalled the great texts of Scripture that spoke of the workings of the great *Ruach* of God.

While every human being possessed the Spirit, the Scriptures pointed to a time, the last age of the world, when God would infuse his Spirit to a degree and extent unknown before. This would be the age of the Messiah when the fullness of the Spirit and the Power of God would be poured out on the world. The prophet Ezechiel had spoken of this coming Spirit in terms of a "heart transplant" that would completely change the nature of each person:

> A new heart I will give to you, and a new spirit I will put within you (36:26).

The prophet Joel had also spoken of these coming last days in terms of a great outpouring of the Spirit that would transform the entire world:

> Afterward I will pour out my spirit upon all flesh. Your sons and daughters shall prophesy, your old men shall dream dreams, your young men shall see visions; even upon the men servants and the maiden-servants in those days I will pour out my spirit (Joel 2:28-29).

Yet the divine plan of God in the Scriptures also pointed to a chosen intermediary as a unique bearer of the Spirit and a special instrument to bring this Spirit to others. The words addressed to Jesus at his baptism (my beloved in whom I am well pleased) reminded him of the prophet Isaiah who had foretold that a future Servant of the Lord would bring the Spirit to the world:

> Behold my servant whom I uphold, my chosen in whom my soul delights; I have put my spirit upon him, he shall bring forth justice to the nations . . . (42:1).

Jesus also remembered Isaiah's promise that the future gift of the Spirit would be an abiding gift that would remain upon a chosen descendant of David:

> There shall come forth a shoot from the stump of Jesus and a branch shall grow out of his roots and the spirit of the Lord shall rest upon him (11:1).

Jesus knew that what he had received at his baptism was not a private gift for him alone. In the bible, when great men of the past had received important revelations — people like Abraham, Moses and the prophets — these were given for the benefit of all the people. Jesus' baptism had confirmed for him personally what John was preaching — the Kingdom of God was at hand, and the New Age was beginning. This meant that God himself was about to inaugurate his rule on earth as king by intervening in world history in a unique manner.

The inauguration of even an earthly king or president is not a secret matter. Since it affects the rest of the world, all other governments must be notified so they can send representatives to the inauguration. Jesus knew that if the kingdom of God was imminently at hand, it must be made known to the whole world, but first to his own people. Time was running out and it was a matter of great urgency. Jesus felt that he must make new priorities for his life. One thing was absolutely certain: the kingdom of God and its proclamation must receive absolute precedence over every family tie or personal obligation. Important decisions must be made very soon about his whole direction of life. His career could be no longer limited to being the carpenter of Nazareth. The urgency of the coming kingdom demanded a fulltime commitment.

Jesus began to reflect, "What does this kingdom of God mean?" He began to shudder with fear as a first answer formulated itself in his mind. Yes, he could not avoid it: there must be a hard-fought hand-to-hand struggle with Satan and the powers of darkness. These present rulers of the world must be overcome and dislodged before God could be king over the world. The task was a frightening one. Ever since the fall and sin of Adam and Eve, the bible bore witness to a world of suffering, crime, violence and sin. This was not chaotic and by chance; there was a definite power and movement of evil masterminded by Satan who worked in human hearts to accomplish his purpose of frustrating the design of God. The kingdom could not come without casting out Satan and his cohorts. Later Jesus would repeat again and again these words, "If I cast out devils by the Spirit of God, then the Kingdom of God has overtaken you" (Matthew 12:28).

If these were, indeed, the last times predicted by the prophets, then this would be a final battle of the forces of evil — a terrible, earthshaking struggle demanding every ounce of strength and courage the Spirit could give him. Should he be like John the Baptist and the members of the dedicated community of Jewish monks, who lived at a place called Qumran, near the Dead Sea? The latter were a religious commune who shared an intense ascetic life combined with a most perfect keeping of the Law, along with prolonged practices of prayer, fasting and renunciation. Many of these people, (only men are mentioned in their Rule) regarded themselves as soldiers in the great final battle between the forces of good and evil. In fact, one of their favorite books was called, "The War of the Sons of Light with the Sons of Darkness."

Some of the ascetic members of the Qumran community had taken upon themselves a life of celibacy. This was because they regarded themselves as soldiers in God's Holy War against the forces of evil. In the bible, even the ordinary soldier of Israel was obliged to refrain from sex even with his wife during times of military service or war. This was a sacred custom that had the force of law. Before a battle, soldiers were told that if they had been newly married, and not yet begun to live with their wives, they could leave at once and go home (Deuteronomy 20:7). The custom was based on the idea that engagement in a Holy War was so close a dedication and consecration to God that the use of sex (although good in itself) might take a person from the complete commitment to God demanded by military service. Jesus might have thought very seriously about this. Would not his absolute dedication to the kingdom of God and the struggle against the forces of evil mean that a wife and family were not to be for him? This was an agonizing decision for him to face.

And then another thought troubled him. The gift of the abiding presence of the Spirit had made him like the temple, the place where the Holy Ark of God was kept. Because the Ark was the special place of God's presence, no one could come near or touch it, except the High Priest who once a year sprinkled it with the blood of sacrifice, and then only with the greatest of fear. All the priests of the temple who officiated at sacrifices had to maintain celibacy during their time of service. This was because participation in sex, according to the Law, resulted in a period of "uncleanness" until sunset (Leviticus 15:18). This "uncleanness" involved nothing of a moral or hygenic nature. It simply meant the person was disqualified from taking part in worship or religious gatherings. This total absorption in worship or service to God had a long history. Even when God gave the Ten Commandments to Moses on Mount Sinai, he ordered all the people were to abstain from sex for three days before, and to wash their garments (Exodus 19:15).

Jesus asked himself, "Would not the need for dedicated worship and attention to the Spirit within me indicate a life of celibacy, like that of a person with the Ark of God continually before him?" This along with the continence demanded of a soldier in God's final Holy War seemed to almost demand a life in which women were to be kept at a distance.

During all this time, unseen powers were carefully watching the young carpenter from Nazareth. Ever since John the Baptist began his ministry, these spirits had detected a new turn in human events. And now in this young man from Nazareth, the dark powers saw something they had never seen before. There had been some signs, in strange occurrences near the Jordan, that this Jesus was the greatest adversary they had faced since the dawn of history. There was no time for delay. Jesus would become more and more aware of his powers. The time to act was now, and the Prince of Darkness himself took on the task.

4. THE PRINCE OF DARKNESS AND THE MYSTERY OF THE DOVE

The Dark Master patiently waited for the most propitious time. Toward the end of the forty days without eating or drinking, Jesus' body would be thoroughly weakened. The oppressive heat and the heavy atmosphere of the lowest valley on earth would hasten the process. As Jesus weakened, the thin balance between conscious and unconscious would gradually disappear, leaving him especially vulnerable to hallucinations, and wide-awake visions. His will would lose its strength to choose; his intellect would not easily discern the delicate shades that so often separate good and evil.

Satan knew which cards to play. Through millions of years of experience, the devil knew all the inner workings of human nature. Most people rejected out-and-out evil: it was so evident and hideous. Few, however, could resist temptation under the guise of what seemed good and even the very will of God. The Prince of Darkness knew the Scriptures well, and it was from there that he drew arguments that few people were able to see through. He was ready to play his first card.

This first card had usually been enough throughout history.

26

He could count on his hands the few people able to resist it. It was the temptation of Power — and was not Power one of the principal attributes of YHWH himself, who was called God almighty, the God of hosts? As Jesus was wrestling with the nature of his role of liberator, what better image was there than that of Moses? Moses was the divinely chosen liberator of the oppressed people of Israel thirteen centuries before when they were humbled slaves of Egypt, the most powerful nation on earth. God gave Moses great signs to prove himself first before the Pharaoh of Egypt and then before his people. Before Pharaoh, Moses had worked three signs: he had changed his staff into a serpent; he had changed the color of the skin on his hand to that of a leper, and then back again; finally he had taken water from the Nile River, and then poured it on the land where it changed into blood (Exodus 4:1-9). In a great act of power, Moses called ten plagues upon the whole Egypt, the final one being the death of all their first-born children. It was a humbled and broken Pharaoh of Egypt who finally allowed the Israelites to leave his land.

However, the greatest sign took place on the Sinai peninsula when they found themselves without food and threatened by starvation. The people were so desperate that they wished they had died in Egypt and had never followed Moses. At this time Moses prayed to God, who replied,

> I have heard the murmurings of the people of Israel; say to them, at twilight you shall eat flesh, and in the morning you shall be filled with bread; then you shall know that I the LORD, am your God (Exodus 16:12).

If Jesus was to be the leader of his people, like Moses, he must show a similar sign to the people. What better sign than to duplicate what Moses had done? It was almost absurd to think that a great liberator of Israel would only lead them to inner liberation from sin, and not to full national liberation from Rome and its power. Was not the Messiah to "bring justice to the nations"? (Isaiah 42:1) How could this be done without breaking the power of Rome? Just as Assyria, Babylonia, Persia, and Greece had fallen by the intervention and power of God, so must Rome.

Matthew describes Jesus' temptation in this way:

> The tempter came and said to him, "If you are the Son of God command these stones to become loaves of bread" (4:3).

Jesus however replied, "Man shall not live by bread alone but by every word that proceeds from the mouth of God" (4:4). In other words, bread and external signs are not sufficient to bring people to God. It is the creative word of God that makes bread and all nourishment possible. This is what people must listen to if they wish to get real nourishment. An inner conversion and obedience is necessary.

This was exactly what John the Baptist had called for. He had worked no sign or miracle externally. But he had effected the greatest miracle of all, the inner conversion necessary for the coming of the kingdom of God. By rejecting Satan's temptation to political power, Jesus, like the Baptist, made a separation between nation/power/state and the kingdom of God that had rarely been made before. The connection between religion and politics had brought about the downfall of David, the first king of Israel and many kings after him.

The Dark Master then tried his second card, one that had rarely failed in all history since it touched the deepest longing in every man's heart, that for the companionship of woman, children and family. Once again Satan built his argument on the Scriptures, where God's plan for man, woman and the world were found. These words were not regarded as stories from ancient history but as instruction for all time — instructions that Jesus had heard again and again in his home and synagogue. Had not the LORD God said when he created man and woman (and his word was Law), "It is not good that man should be alone; I will make a helper fit for him" (Genesis 2:18)? To marry and raise a family was a religious command that came from God himself. Jesus saw how different this was from the world of John the Baptist. It was a man's world, and John had male disciples. The few women who came to him at the Jordan returned to their homes. The devil delicately suggested, "Why should you be so different from everyone else, without a family, without the warmth and companionship of a wife and children? Is it not pride to set yourself up as someone different — as above the command of God himself in the Holy Scriptures?"

The texts of Scripture came one after another to Jesus' mind. It was God himself who had shared his own powers of creation with the human race and actually *commanded* them to make use of it:

> God created man in his own image; in the image of God he created him; male and female he created them. God blessed and God said to them, "Be fruitful and multiply, and fill the earth and subdue it" (1:28).

An old story was told again and again by later Rabbis, was perhaps told even in Jesus time:

> A Roman lady asked a rabbi, "How many days did it take the Holy One, blessed be He, to create the universe?": The rabbi answered, "In six days." The lady then asked, "What has God been doing ever since that time?" The rabbi answered, "He has been arranging marriages."

In fact, the very means by which procreation should take

place was carefully planned by God. Jesus had heard often in the synagogue an explanation of the deep symbolic sense of Genesis 2:21-22:

> So the LORD God caused a deep sleep to fall upon the man and while he was asleep, took one of his ribs and closed up its place with flesh. And the rib which the Lord God had taken from the man, he made into a woman.

This symbolic sense, explained in mysterious undertones was that there was something missing in man that could be supplied by woman as they united together in the embrace of marriage. God himself had made them to "fit" together in this way. And when they did, they became no longer two but one flesh as the text further explains:

> Therefore a man leaves his father and his mother and cleaves to his wife, and they become one flesh (Genesis 2:24).

Weakened as his body was through fasting, one vivid image after another came to Jesus' imagination, almost overwhelming him with their power. He may have thought of the young woman his parents had selected for him as a marriage partner. He hardly knew her. In those days young men and women did not speak alone together and even the opportunities to do so were rare. The image of her face now became more vivid and real than in any time in his life. He saw himself beside her in the deep sleep of the Genesis text, fulfilling the holy command of God. The word Adam (man) came from the word Adamah (earth) because he was taken from the earth (Genesis 2:19). Through the woman, he saw himself return to the feminine mother earth once more. His face pressed against hers; her chest and the nourishing breasts of mother earth were against his. The missing rib now made them one as their loins touched one another, he entering into her and she encompassing and encircling him. "And the two of them became one flesh."

For Jesus and his people, the marriage union was not only commanded by God, but was also an image and reminder of God's own union with his people. The Scriptures, in most vivid terms, wrote of God's union with his people in terms of the sexual union of man and woman. Ezechiel had written of God and Israel in these words: God said,

> You grew up and became tall and arrived at full maidenhood: you came to the age of puberty; your breasts were formed, your hair had grown; yet you were naked and bare. Again I passed by you and saw that you were now old enough for love. So I spread the corner of my cloak over you to cover your nakedness: I swore an oath to you and entered into a covenant with you and you became mine . . . (16:7-8).

The prophet Hosea also wrote how God spoke to his people as if to his own bride with these words:

> I will betroth you to me forever: I will betroth you in righteousness and in justice, in steadfast love and in mercy;

What more beautiful way to remember God and his relationship to his people than through this inner meaning of the marriage union! God himself was the author of this covenant. It was sacred and holy, a reminder of his own presence, covenant and marriage bond with his people.

Exhausted and weakened as he was, Jesus felt a sense of guilt: how could he go against the very command of God in the Scriptures? Not only that — how beautiful, holy and sacred was the companionship and union between man and woman, with its delights planned by God himself. Why should he condemn himself to a lonely life, like that of John the Baptist with his cold, ascetic ways and frequent fastings? Jesus could see no way out except to return to Nazareth. His marriage would not impede his dedication to God; it would even enhance it and strengthen it.

Jesus took a deep breath. And as he did, the *dove* image of the Holy Spirit/Breath of God that he saw coming down from the sky at his baptism filled his imagination once more. At this moment he received a sudden insight as to the meaning of the dove at the moment of his baptism. The dove in biblical tradition had always been a very special symbol of love. The mating patterns of doves as well as their gentleness and innocence had always attracted the Hebrews. Often lovers and spouses called one another by the name "dove." In that beautiful collection of love poems called, The Song of Songs, the bride says to her spouse, "Open to me, my sister, my love, my dove, my perfect one" (5:2). The Targum (an Aramaic translation of the Hebrew Bible) on the verse of the Song of Songs, "The voice of the dove is heard in our land" (2:2) interpreted this as the voice of the Holy Spirit.

Jesus felt a burning sensation in his heart as the full implications of the dove vision at his baptism came to him. The Holy Spirit in the form of a dove was a powerful image of an inner marriage taking place at the depths of his being. The feminine *Ruach* (breath, spirit) of God was uniting herself to him in the most intimate possible manner. The Scripture text in Ezechiel and Hoseah that described a marriage of God with his people had now become a concrete reality within him through his experience of the Dove-Spirit coming upon him and remaining with him.

Suddenly Jesus felt a great peace within him. The inner conflict caused by the Genesis texts beginning with "It is not good for man to be alone" (2:18) stopped tormenting him. These texts had spoken of a need, a necessity, a command in view of the needs that every person ordinarily felt. But now this was the New Age. Jesus no longer felt marriage was commanded by God, for he experienced the inner marriage of the Spirit, the source of all earthly marriages. This would mean not avoiding women, or dismissing them from his life. On the contrary it meant a new freedom: he could love them truly *for themselves,* much more than *for himself.* It did not mean that he would not marry, but that it was his free choice to do so or not in view of his mission of the proclamation of the kingdom of God. In fact, he saw dimly in the future that a new collaboration and association with women would be possible in the New Age.

Then Jesus remembered his first inclination to imitate John the Baptist and many of the monks of Qumran in regard to their vow of celibacy in view of the ancient soldier's commitment to avoid sex in time of war against the powers of darkness. He remembered the comparison of his own body to the Temple and Ark of God, with all the taboos of sex that were connected to this. But Jesus smiled. After all, these were customs and prescriptions from the past. A New Age had begun, and the past was over. His only consideration now must be the Kingdom of God, and the future.

Jesus then returned to John the Baptist at the Jordan. He was no longer tired and exhausted. He did not need to command that stones become bread in order to nourish him; he was now sustained by the inner creative Word of God, the source of all bread and nourishment. On the other side, Satan the Dark Master, had not finished with Jesus. He still had a trump card in his hand which he would play at the appointed time.

Jesus spent the next few months working with the Baptist by the Jordan and learning many things from him. John was the most sincere and conscientious man he had ever met, the example of total dedication to God. At a later date Jesus would say, "Amen I say to you, among those born of women there has risen no one greater than John the Baptist" (Matthew 11:11). John himself was a strict vegetarian, for his food of wild locusts

was not considered meat. He drew his inspiration for this practice from the words of God in the creation story, where God
gave to the animals and to all human beings fruits and green
plants for food (1:29-30). This is why there had been no violence
in creation in the garden of Eden, for the animals (being likewise
vegetarians) would not harm one another.

It was only after the great flood that God "reluctantly" permitted animals to be killed for sacrifice and for food, but it was
not regarded as the ideal (Genesis 9:3-6). John felt that the
New Age of the Kingdom of God was at hand; the earth must
become once again like the garden of paradise. The kingdom
of God must be a world of justice and peace once more. The
prophet Isaiah had spoken of such a world to come and the
Baptist wished to bring it about here and now by a delicate
sensitivity to all life.

The followers of the Baptist imitated their master. He taught
them special mantras or formulas of prayer. Definite spiritual
practices meant a great deal to his disciples. Later some disciples of Jesus asked him to perform the same function: "Lord,
teach us to pray, as John taught his disciples" (Luke 11:1).
John also taught them to fast frequently to strengthen their
wills to total dedication to God. In fact, many people who later
listened to Jesus were disappointed that Jesus did not teach
the rigorous asceticism of the Baptist. They said to him, "Why
do John's disciples and those of the Pharisees fast while yours
do not?" (Mark 2:18). For many people in Jerusalem, the Baptist
was a fanatic, a religious madman. Later Jesus would say,
"John appeared neither eating nor drinking, and people say,
'He is mad!' " (Matthew 11:18).

The Baptist grew to appreciate more and more the unusual
caliber of the young carpenter from Nazareth. He recognized
his special ability and asked him to cooperate in his chosen
work of baptizing repentant sinners in preparation for the kingdom of God. Jesus along with his disciples began to baptize

also in another region near the Jordan River. He followed the leadership of the Baptist. He stayed in one spot where people could come, even from far off, remain a while, listen to his teachings and be baptized. Here was a spiritual oasis from which you could come and go, returning with renewal to your place in the world. Only a very few actually stayed any length of time with Jesus or the Baptist. For Jesus, this became more and more disturbing. There were great limitations on the people they could reach: what about the aged, the poor, the sick? Then too, what about women? Only a very few were able to make this long trip to the Jordan. The world of the Baptist was strictly a man's world with 50% of the population effectively eliminated. For Jesus, an answer to this difficulty was soon to come in a very unexpected manner: the Baptist was arrested one day by Herod's soldiers and thrown into prison.

When the news of the Baptist's arrest — a prelude to his later death — came to Jesus, he was faced with another great decision. Many of the former disciples of the Baptist gathered at his side looking for guidance. A keen sense of the urgency of time came to Jesus. If John was arrested, it was logical that Jesus as his successor might be arrested and even executed within a short time. He must make the best possible use of the limited time left to bring about the repentance of Israel in view of the coming kingdom.

Jesus had a sense of impending doom and urgency as he saw the direction that his country was going. There was a growing underground movement against Rome, and the guerrillas had much popular support. It did not matter if Rome was the mightiest nation on earth; God himself would fight their battles, for religion and nation were inseparably united. Did God bring the Jews out of Egypt by only inner repentance? No, through power and mighty signs the great liberation of Israel from Egypt had taken place. Also, did not God enable David, their first king, to lead their soldiers in victory over their Philistine oppressors?

The whole period of time around the ministry of Jesus was

a history of this growing resistance. Even before his birth there had been a great rebellion in Galilee in which a certain Judas had sought to become the Jewish king. This event and other outbreaks caused Varus the Roman commander of Syria to bring two legions and four troops of cavalry to Palestine. At this time over 2000 revolutionaries were executed.

Although the military underground movement was powerful, it was really the work of a small minority. Nevertheless, most people sympathized with it. But there was always a danger that it could suddenly erupt in a massive stubborn revolution if the general public were sufficiently disturbed. Jesus had recently received alarming news about the new Roman Governor Pontius Pilate. When Pilate arrived in Jerusalem in 26 A.D., he infuriated the Jews when his troops carried army standards with Roman images of the gods. This was particularly offensive to the Jews, whose first commandment forbade any such images. Crowds of Jews followed Pilate even as far as his headquarters in Caesarea. Josephus relates that many Jews even bared their necks before the Roman swords preferring to die rather than see the Law broken. Pilate finally agreed to remove the religious standards, used in Roman sacrifices, from Jerusalem.

A short time afterward, Pilate confiscated money in the Jewish temple. This was regarded as sacred money only to be used for the temple building and maintenance. It was completely abhorrent to Jews that pagan Gentiles should touch this money. Mobs of Jews assembled in protest. Pilate had his soldiers concealed in the crowds in civilian robes, with swords and clubs concealed beneath their garments. At the proper time, they took out their weapons and subdued the crowds through a bloody massacre. It seems to be this occasion that Jesus refers to in the gospel of Luke when he speaks of Galileans whose blood Pilate had mixed with their sacrifices (13:1).

Jesus watched these signs of approaching revolt against Rome with great anxiety. Little time remained for him to emphasize that the first step in the liberation of Israel was not military action but repentance and conversion. Rome was a terrible oppressor, but the most important enemy to be overcome was the oppressor within each person. John the Baptist, it is true, had emphasized this inner repentance, but had by no means eliminated the possibility that the Messiah might intervene and act with political power also. John had said, "He who is coming after me is more powerful than I" (Matthew 1:11). Later in prison, John had sent messengers to Jesus asking, "Are you he who is to come, or shall we look for another?" (3:11) Perhaps John was waiting for Jesus to finally show the great acts of power that would definitely point to him as the awaited liberator of Israel.

Pressed by the urgency of these events, Jesus came to very important decisions. Time would not permit him to remain by the Jordan and baptize those repentant sinners who came to him. He must reach as many people as possible, in as many ways as he could. He must return to Galilee and begin a nation-wide tour of Israel to bring the message of repentance and the coming of the kingdom of God. The gospels point to John's arrest, and the return of Jesus to Galilee as the start of his public ministry to the nation (Matthew 4:2; Mark 1:14).

As Jesus walked back to Galilee with Peter, Andrew, James and John, former disciples of the Baptist, there were other pressing decisions he had to make about his whole approach, which would be distinct from the Baptist. With the urgency of time due to the arrest of the Baptist and the growing possibility of revolt against Rome, how would this fit into the marriage planned by his parents? He meditated and searched the Scriptures and perhaps found a model in the prophet Jeremiah who faced a similar historical situation: Babylon was the oppressor of Israel in the years before 587 B.C., the destruction of Jerusalem. Jeremiah had counseled the king, the leaders and priests not to fight a useless war against Babylon for he knew it would only lead to the destruction of his country. He had this conviction as the result of a message of God, who told him not to marry to signify that destruction was imminent if they kept their trust in the military, and not in their covenant with God. God had told Jeremiah, "Do not marry any woman; you shall not have sons or daughters in this place" (Jeremiah 16:1). This order was given because families and small children would face horrible suffering at the hands of the Babylonians. Jeremiah's celibacy was to be a sign to all the people that destruction was imminent unless there was radical change. Jesus decided that he would follow the same path as Jeremiah, and made this resolve in his heart.

5. THE MOTHER AND THE FAMILY

As Jesus returned to Galilee from the Jordan he kept deliberating this important question: How completely should he break away from the Baptist's approach? Once again he turned to the Scriptures for inspiration. The supreme path for every true Jew and son of God was to imitate God. To be a true son was to be like God, and to act as he did. This God was not a God of philosophy but a God who was with his people, a God whose actions could be watched and imitated.

In this matter of imitation, Jesus often thought of the craftsman's parable,

> The son can do nothing of his own accord, but only what he sees the father doing; for whatever he does, that the son does likewise. For the father loves the son and shows him all that he himself is doing (John 5:19-20).

Joseph his father often recalled this parable. But Jesus learned it more by action than by words. Trades and professions were handed down in the family from father to son. If someone remarked that Jesus was the son of Joseph or the son of the

39

carpenter, it would be taken for granted that Jesus would be a carpenter also, for trade skills were family secrets transmitted from generation to generation. In Joseph's carpenter shop, Jesus watched, imitated and learned the trade that would support himself and his future family. As a loving father, Joseph delighted in teaching him all he knew.

Yet Jesus knew God was above every human father, and that to imitate him was the highest goal a human being could reach. The most moving image of God for every Jew was that of a Liberator. As a prelude to the Ten Commandments God had said, "I am the Lord, your God, who brought you out of the land of Egypt" (Exodus 20:1). This YHWH had taken the first step, the actual initiative to save his people when they were helpless slaves of the Pharaoh. Appearing to Moses in the burning bush, God said, "I have seen the affliction of my people who are in Egypt . . . and have come down to deliver them out of the land of the Egyptians" (Exodus 3:7). Jesus was especially moved by the quality of *grace,* that beautiful quality of initiative so characteristic of God. This must be an essential element of his own ministry, but how?

As Jesus was walking along he saw a shepherd leading a flock of sheep. His favorite passage of Scripture flashed into his mind, the one found in the 34th chapter of Ezechiel. Here God compares himself, as the true shepherd of his people, to the ordinary shepherds and leaders of Israel. God says,

> Ho, shepherds of Israel who have been feeding yourselves! Should not shepherds feed the sheep? You eat the fat, you clothe yourselves with the wool, you slaughter the fatlings; but you do not feed the sheep (34:2-3).

The picture here is that of any shepherd — of course they take care of sheep so they can wear their wool and eat their lamb chops! What else? Yet God as a shepherd far surpasses any human leader. He takes care of his people, his sheep, not for himself but for themselves. He *cares* for his sheep. So Ezechiel announces, speaking in the name of God:

> I myself will search for my sheep and seek them out
> . . . I will rescue them from all places where they
> have been scattered on a day of clouds and thick
> darkness . . . I will seek the lost . . . I will bring
> back the strayed . . . I will bind up the crippled . . .
> I will strengthen the weak . . . I will feed them in
> justice (34:11-16).

Jesus' eyes became moist as he recalled this tender image of God going out to seek his lost sheep, caring for the injured, and healing the sick ones. It was a most precious model of God's grace and initiative. If he, Jesus, was to be a real *liberator* of his people, he must *go out* as God did to the lost and wounded sheep of Israel, the abandoned ones that no one wanted. Who were these outcasts of Israel to whom he must go? He saw their faces in his imagination. They were those commonly regarded as outside the Law. They were the hated tax-collectors, those whose cooperation made Roman oppression possible. They were the "sinners," whose way of life, or even occupation made them suspect in the eyes of the just. They were those who were sick, because this was usually considered the result of some transgression or sin. Many of these sicknesses also made them "unclean" in the eyes of the Law, meaning they could not take part in social and religious gatherings. Most pitiful were those afflicted with mental ailments, commonly regarded as possessed by evil spirits. Then there were the Gentiles themselves who were also regarded as unclean. And finally, there were women who were the great oppressed half of the population (cf. next chapter).

Jesus could not wait for them to come to him, as did the Baptist. Like God, he must take the first step of grace and go out to them where they were. He could not, like the community of Qumran or the Pharisee religious leaders, wait for them to be converted and become perfect observers of the Law. This would be a conditional love. He must go out to them, taking the initiative of finding them and accepting them as they are. Only in this way would they know the unconditional love and forgiveness of God himself. Jesus knew this was the only way for him. But he now envisioned a double danger before him: First his mission would bring him in sharp conflict with Herod and Rome. Second, it would bring him into direct confrontation with the powerful religious leaders of his country. Jesus shuddered to think about how his family would react to this aspect of his mission.

As Jesus approached Nazareth, he could almost predict word for word the reaction of his family, especially his mother. He knew them too well. As for his mother, it is hard to imagine stronger ties between two human beings. He was, of course, her unique firstborn son. The impressions conveyed by a first child are so striking and new that no other child can possibly duplicate them. But in Jewish custom, there were much deeper connections. The firstborn was considered, "the one that opens the womb" — a special miracle of God. The firstborn son also received a double portion of the family inheritance. In addition, he took on a role of supervision over the other children, and after the death of the father inherited all of his authority. In ancient times the firstborn son was consecrated as a priest to God. When the tribe of Levi took the place of the firstborn sons, each newlyborn son was still offered to God as a priest, but was "bought back" by an offering and sacrifice, forty days after the child was born (Luke 2:23). Mary had told Jesus in detail about this dramatic moment in her life, when she went to the temple to present her firstborn child as a priestly offering to God, and then take him back.

In addition, Jesus and his mother shared a special secret that no one else except Joseph knew about. When Jesus was

a child, Mary had whispered to him the story of an angel of
God announcing to her that she would conceive a child through
the work of the Holy Spirit. And this all came to pass after she
was engaged to Joseph, during the customary time they waited
before coming to live together. Mary never mentioned this
again, but Jesus often caught a glance of her eyes in which he
read that the mysterious secret was a unique bond between
them.

It was Mary who was the great teacher of his life. She had
instructed him in all the details that went into a dedicated
life-style according to the Torah. It was not until after twelve
years of age that Jesus spent more and more time in Joseph's
workshop; but his training in the Law had already been completed by then. The most precious heritage his mother had
given him was a deep consciousness and awareness of the Spirit
in all of life. She had taught him the little secret of awareness
of his breathing as a means of a deeper awareness of the Holy
Breath of God. She told him stories like that of Elisha the
prophet who was so confident in the divine energy in his breathing that he raised a dead young boy to life by directly breathing
into his mouth: "Then he went up and lay upon the child,
putting his mouth upon the child's mouth, his eyes upon the
eyes, and his hands upon the hands" (2 Kings 4:34). Mary also
reminded Jesus that Daniel had spoken of God as the one "in
whose hand is your breath and whose are all your ways" (5:23).

Jesus rehearsed his coming meeting with his family again
and again, but the total emotional impact could not possibly
come upon him at once. When he reached home, he was greeted
with joyous affection by everyone. They felt that now his stint
with the Baptist was finished. He would now take up his career
as a carpenter, settle down, raise a family and do all that was
expected of a God-fearing Jewish young man.

When he told them he was determined to continue the Baptist's mission, but on a broader scale, they were stunned. His

mother instinctively placed her hand over her heart as if she had been pierced with a sword (cf. Luke 2:35). Jesus could almost see in her eyes the frightening image that was in her mind. Even before Jesus was born, and during his childhood, thousands of young Israelites had been nailed to Roman crosses with their blood drenching the fields of Galilee. She knew that King Herod would seek to destroy him, just as he had already planned to destroy the Baptist. Jesus would be next on the list. If Herod did not do so, it would certainly be Roman soldiers who would carry him off to be crucified. The Romans knew that religion and nation went together. Jesus' open proclamation of a coming kingdom would be enough for them. After all, the kingdom is a realm — a place where a Jewish king or Messiah would rule. Jesus' gathering of disciples and public support would constitute a serious threat and danger to Rome. The Romans would not be able to neatly distinguish that Jesus wanted an inner kingdom.

Jesus' family marshaled every possible intellectual and emotional argument to sway Jesus from his decision. The hardest one to bear was the continual description of the agonizing suffering this would bring upon his mother, and the family. If Jesus were the only one concerned, he could well make his own decision. But this was one that affected every member of the family. It was a direct threat to the whole meaning of their lives and eventually to their life itself. For if Herod or the Romans sought to seize Jesus, who would be next on their list? Of course it would be his brothers and sisters, his mother, and relatives. Who else?

Jesus could not stand for this for more than a few days. The high pitch of emotion was too much for him to bear. He left Nazareth with his disciples and moved to Capernaum, near Lake Galilee, where he stayed at the house of Peter, one of John's former disciples. This became his new home. Jesus was close to a state of shock for some days. He now felt a great barrier between himself and his family, the people he had known and loved the most of his life. Most of all he had lost, at least for a time, the dearest person in his life, his own mother. Indeed the women in his life had been his mother and his sisters, and now there was no one.

Jesus spent considerable time training the former disciples of John, and choosing new ones. This work was a most important one, for Jesus' closest collaborators were not only to preach the kingdom, but were to live it, following his own life-style. They were to be a kingdom in miniature — a living model of what they preached. Jesus had already determined that his mission would be concentrated on the lost sheep of the tribe of Israel, and the members of the inner group should reflect this. In doing so he made a choice that shocked the former disciples of the Baptist and even brought him undying opposition from every religious leader in Galilee.

One day he was walking along the sea of Galilee and passed by a tax booth where duties were collected on all trade coming in and out of Galilee. Levi, the son of Alphaeus, was manning the tax office when Jesus came by. Levi was a rich man. The office of tax collector was the most rewarding position a Jew could obtain under Roman government. Levi had bought the position at a great price, since it was farmed out by the Romans to the highest bidder. Passersby often spat in his direction and cursed him, for he was a puppet of the foreign oppressor, making his money through collecting the exorbitant taxes imposed by Rome. He was not welcome in the synagogue or any public gathering, for he was regarded as permanently unclean because of his continual commerce with Gentiles and foreigners. He was truly a religious and social outcast.

Jesus entered directly into Levi's office and called him, saying "Follow me." Levi was completely overcome by Jesus' acceptance of him, and his unconditional forgiveness of all the wrongs and cheating he had done. He left his tax-collector's booth and became part of the inner circle of Jesus' disciples. To celebrate this, he threw a great party to which he invited all his friends among whom were many tax collectors like himself and "sinners." We can imagine nothing that would so enrage the religious leaders of the area. Many of them were Pharisees, strictest of strict when it came to the Law. And here was Jesus posing as a religious teacher yet with a disciple who had openly disregarded the Law and had even cooperated with the Gentiles in cheating his people. Not only that, Jesus was enjoying a loud and merry party with Levi and his friends. The scribes confronted the disciples of Jesus and asked, "Why does your teacher eat with tax collectors and sinners?" Jesus heard this and replied, "I came not to call the righteous, but sinners" (Matthew 9:13).

The implications of this were immediately understood by the Scribes and Pharisees. The call to the kingdom of God was open to repentant sinners, but not to them, since obviously they did not need repentance. This was a threat not only to their position of authority among the people, but even to their whole life-style. It was too much for them to bear. From that time on, the opposition of the religious establishment to Jesus became stronger and stronger. What authority did Jesus have for his mission to announce the kingdom of God, and the position he took in regard to the outcasts of Israel? Some of the leaders even secretly approached friends of Herod to discuss what to do about this common threat.

The call of a tax collector also had political connotations. It meant that Jesus' mission as a liberator was not really directed against the Romans, but was directed to healing oppression *within* their country. Jesus did not support the revolutionary movement, which refused to pay taxes or have anything to do with Rome except prepare for a war. This incident gave a definite turn to Jesus' mission as being essentially a peace movement. As such, it would earn the undying opposition of fervent nationalists, and make it hard for him to gain a large popular following.

Meanwhile the family of Jesus had by no means forgotten

about him. They were becoming more embarrassed day by day. Jesus' confrontation with their own religious teachers made many people raise their eyes at them in the synagogue or make cutting remarks to them on the streets. Some action must be taken, and it seems that they resolved to somehow force Jesus to stop. They picked a time when Jesus was teaching in a house, surrounded by his disciples and a large group of people. It was the family's fear that Jesus had perhaps gone out of his mind, and that it was their duty to protect him from doing harm to himself and others.

On this occasion, the mother herself took the leadership, surrounded by Jesus' four brothers. They went to the house and sent a message inside that Jesus was to come out. And they meant it. No son could ever say *no* to such a parental order. The message came to Jesus: "Your mother and your brothers are outside, asking for you" (Mark 3:32). When the message was announced, everyone expected Jesus to immediately go out to them. Instead, they were surprised when he slowly turned to those around him, and said, "Who are my mother and brothers?" Then he gazed at the older women, and the younger men and women, looking them deliberately in the eye while he said, "Here are my mother and my brothers! Whoever does the will of God is my brother and sister, and mother" (Mark 3:34-35).

The gospel does not describe the reaction of Jesus' mother and family to this statement. For his mother, such a reply was a terrible shock. Jesus had told her that his new family meant more to him than they did: the women in the house were now his mother and sisters; the men were now his brothers. They walked sadly away. And Jesus was sad also when he thought about it. In his preaching later on, he would recall this moment and sadly say to his disciples that the call to the kingdom must take precedence over every family tie:

If anyone comes to me and does not hate his own

father and mother and wife and children and
brothers and sisters, yes and even his own life, he
cannot be my disciple (Luke 14:26).

The word "hate" in this text does not refer to anger or resent-
ment but the ability to suffer deep pain of separation in agonizing decisions about family that may have to be made.

Yet, deep in his heart, Jesus knew the separation from his
mother was only external. There was an inner communion and
trust between the two of them that nothing could destroy. He
was perfectly confident that she would continue to play an
important part in his life. She would stand by him at an hour
and time when he needed her most.

Yet, this painful encounter with the family was a freeing
event as well. Jesus had made his decision, and now it was
behind him. In doing so, he had put behind him the women
who had meant the most in his life: his mother and his sisters.
His life was left with a void. But there also had been a great
void in the religious teachings of his time, and even in the
teaching of the Baptist that he had so admired. The great void
was the lack of recognition of the importance of women in the
whole coming great event of the kingdom of God.

6. A WOMAN'S WORLD, ISRAEL, FIRST CENTURY A.D.

A woman's world at that time could be essentially defined in her relationship to a man. Before marriage she belonged to a man, her father, whom she addressed as master or Lord. To him she owed absolute obedience. Like her mother, she was part of the household that essentially belonged to the father. The daughters did not have the same rights as sons. They could own no property, or have any part in an inheritance, unless there were no sons. Even personally, she was subject to her father, not being able to make vows or contracts, buy or sell without his permission. Whatever earnings she made belonged to him.

In the home, the essential role of the daughter was to assist the other women of the house in their special work of caring for the children and serving the men. In the personal realm of nurture and care, the woman was supreme. She was the first teacher of her children. Household duties were heavy and time-consuming. The daily duty to prepare fresh bread began long before dawn with the heavy chore of grinding the wheat into flour, preparing the flour for baking, kneading it, giving it time to rise, and then baking it. Then the nursing of small children was a constant interruption for they were nursed at the breast until about two years old. The clothes of the family were the women's special responsibility. The cloth had to be first woven from thread, then cut, and finally sewed.

Women were expected to give special attention to serving both the father/husband and the sons. They prepared their meals and clothes, and often washed their feet when they came inside the house from a dusty or muddy road. They anointed their heads and body with oil when their skins were dry and parched from working in the sun. It was the special duty of the wife to prepare her husband's cup, and attend to his needs.

Marriage

A young woman's marriage was arranged by her parents at a very young age, sometimes less than twelve years old. The betrothal was actually arranged in the form of a contract, with payment going to the father of the bride. After she was married, it was customary to wait a period of time, sometimes as long as a year before the husband would begin to live with her by coming to take her into his father's house. This would be the time of joyful wedding festivities that would often last for an entire week. Once she came into her husband's house, he became her new master to whom she owed obedience in place of her father. She was also required to be obedient to the older women in the household.

Very few women remained single. Marriage was regarded as the normal state, and there were few things a woman could do outside of the family. Men were allowed to have more than one wife, although this was something only the rich could afford. The fact of even occasional polygamy made it even more likely that practically all women would be married. Divorce was not possible on a woman's initiative. Only a man could divorce a woman. Divorces were not very common, since it would require returning the marriage price. There were two schools of opinion about how serious a reason was required to divorce a wife: the school of Hillel, which was very lenient, and that of Shammai, which required a very serious reason. Absence of children would itself be a serious ground, since this was always blamed on women because of the views on human physiology at the time.

Social Relations and Public Affairs

Only young men were educated in reading and writing, since a woman's place was in the home. It was forbidden for a woman to be a teacher. Because of her dependency on either father or husband, the witness of women was not accepted in court, nor could they enter into legal or business contracts. A woman rarely appeared outside the home, except in rural regions where she would assist in agricultural work in the fields. If she did appear outside, it was always with a veil that would shield her face. Only on the day of her wedding would her face be unveiled before the public. Men did not speak to women in public. Even Jesus' disciples on one occasion wondered why he was talking alone with a woman while they had gone off to purchase food (John 4:27). It was men who customarily did the shopping each day or went to market. Women usually went out only to bring home water from the village well several times a day. Here is where most of the local news was exchanged, and where men sometimes came to view (at least from a distance) the women of the town.

Religion and Social Gatherings

These two are together because they are rarely separated. Women did come out publicly to take part in the great religious feasts each year, especially Passover, Pentecost, and Tabernances, each of which was celebrated for a week in Jerusalem. They participated in the rituals and dances at this time, which gave young men the opportunity to see them. Religious Laws had a dramatic effect on women in society at that time. Many laws of "uncleanness" especially affected women. This "clean" or "unclean" category had nothing to do with hygiene or ethics. Some actions, such as burying or touching the dead brought uncleanness, but were actually ordered by the Law and praised as a work of charity. Ritual uncleanness meant that a person could not take part in religious or social gatherings; some types of uncleanness were even contagious — they could be spread to other people by either touching them or articles that had been touched by them.

Many of these "taboos" were concerning blood. The Hebrews and many ancients connected blood with the source of all life and fertility. Hence it was especially sacred, belonging to God, who was the author of the life that resided in the blood. Conception was considered to take place by the reaction of a man's seed with the blood in a woman's womb. Blood was considered so sacred that no blood of any animal could ever be consumed. Every animal had to be reverently slaughtered, allowing its blood to go into the ground, and back to God. Women above all were subject to uncleanness in regard to blood. At the time of the birth of a child, they would be ritually unclean for forty days for a male child; eighty days for a daughter. Each month, a woman's period was regarded as a mini-childbirth, because of the mystery of blood. She was then ritually unclean for seven full days. At the end of this period, she underwent a ritual washing. This uncleanness meant a rigid separation from others, since it was considered extremely "contagious." Any article or person she touched became "unclean." Any chair she sat on could bring uncleanness to someone else. Consequently, she had to be apart during this time with special furniture, dishes, etc. (cf. Leviticus 15:19-24). Sexual intercourse during this time was severely prohibited. Women were not allowed in the Temple Area, even the court of the Gentiles at this time. At other times, they could enter the court of women, but not into the court of men, or the court of priests. In the synagogue, women had seats together on one side, or in back. They listened in silence, while the men prayed out loud.

In regard to religious laws, women were obliged to all the negative precepts of the Law, but not those that prescribed positive matters (i.e., specific words and actions). For example, she was not obliged to recite the blessings and prayers that were to be pronounced over foods and at the time of special events. She was not bound to the customary morning and evening prayers, nor was she bound to the study of the Torah as were men. Her special responsibility was to make it possible for men to be truly religious. She did this by providing all the atmosphere necessary in the home, and all the sufficient leisure he needed for the fulfillment of his religious obligations. Even in religion, the role of women was more to assist men.

Some of the ethical prescriptions of the bible had a double standard for men and women. We have already mentioned the matter of divorce. In regard to adultery, both partners were liable to punishment by death. However, even if the woman was only suspected of adultery, she could be required to go through the ordeal of jealousy. This consisted of a drink of holy water mixed with dust along with a solemn oath. If she were guilty, it was believed that her body would swell up in a serious sickness afflicting her womb. If she were innocent, she would be free to conceive children (Numbers 5:12-28). Such an ordeal was not required of men.

Another example of this double standard was that a husband could accuse his wife of not being a virgin before she was married; however, nothing is said in regard to men having sex before marriage. The biblical text reads,

> If a man takes a wife . . . and brings an evil name upon her saying, "I took this woman, and when I came near her, I did not find in her the tokens of virginity" then the father of the young woman and her mother shall take and bring out the tokens to the elders at the city gate (Deuteronomy 22:13-25).

This "tokens of virginity" came from the custom of saving part of the bridal garment or sheet stained with some blood from the first nuptial relationship as a sign that the woman was physically a virgin at the time of marriage. This "evidence" was kept by the parents in case such a future accusation might take place. The modern reader is struck by the flimsiness of this type of evidence.

Women and God

Woman's position under the power of man is a strange paradox. Beneath it all seems to lie a fear of her mysterious and awesome powers. The taboos connected with blood and fertility have their root in her intimate connection with God and divine powers. God himself is the author and source of fertility, birth and creation. And in this matter, woman was closest to the source. Every birth was considered a special miracle. It was a great mystery and God was the one who "opened the womb." The very name given to the first woman — Eve — comes from the Hebrew word for "life." The text notes that Adam called her Eve because she was the mother of all the living (Genesis 3:20). This name describes not only the first woman, but every woman as the source of mysterious life, a source intimately connected with God.

It was in the mother's nourishing and warm womb that life began and was nurtured. It was there the child first felt the meaning of love and care. The Hebrew word for womb was *rechem*. From this root came the most meaningful word for love in the Hebrew language, *rachamim* (tender mercy) and *racham,* the verb to love. The root model for God's own love — which describes his very essence — was taken from the womb-love of a mother, for there it was that God's power worked in a miraculous way. In the bible, when it came to expressing God's love, the strongest image that could be found was that of a mother's love. An example is the favorite text in Isaiah the prophet,

But Zion said, "The Lord has forsaken me; my Lord has forgotten me." Can a mother forget her sucking child, that she should have no compassion on the child in her womb? Even these may forget, yet I will not forget you (49:15).

So it appears that man's efforts to control woman and keep her in a subordinate position were due to her mysterious powers and closeness to God. This is something that belongs to the inner nature of woman. It is something within her that cannot be changed. Any efforts of control or suppression must be from the outside, through power or force. This way was open to man with his superior physical weight and power.

Woman and Sex

There is no separate word for sex in the Hebrew language. Life is sex and sex is life. They are intermingled and interconnected at their roots. Likewise there is no distinction between the word "love," when used of God, and the love that occurs in the most intimate union between man and woman. There are no special words that are used for the sexual organs. The bible thinks more in terms of the total union of persons rather than concentrating on various parts of the body. What today is described as "sexual intercourse" is simply described in the bible as lying down with woman/man. Or the verb "know" is used in a very deep and intimate sense. It is enough for the bible text to say, "Now Adam knew Eve his wife, and she conceived and bore Cain" (Genesis 4:1). God's place in all of this is immediately noted by the woman saying "I have gotten a manchild with the help of the LORD." The nearest the bible comes to naming female sexual organs is to refer to the sexual union in terms of "uncovering the nakedness" of a woman. Or in regard to man, it would be simply "his flesh." Circumcision was described as a cutting of the foreskin of a man's flesh. Or the "feet" might include the lower part of the body, with the word "loins" being more specific, as regards the general area.

There is however a deep feeling in biblical literature that the woman is closer to the earth, and more at one with the plants, animals and all creation than man is. She is rooted to the earth, which is the mother and source of life, just as she is. The idea of "mother earth" goes back many thousands of years. This seems hinted in the story of the creation of the first man and woman. It is the woman who takes the fruit from the tree of knowledge of good and evil that is rooted deeply in the earth. This symbolizes the mysterious powers of sexuality and fertility. She gives the fruit of this tree to man. She it is who draws him and initiates him into the great mysteries of life and fertility as being the one closest to the earth.

In ancient Hebrew literature there is nothing like a marriage or sex manual. It would be unthinkable for them to isolate these matters in such a way. The great book of love was the Song of Songs (or Canticle of Canticles). It was a series of love poems that could have been written about clandestine lovers, or they might even have been wedding songs in which the bride and bridegroom as well as the chorus alternated in singing. While this book was written centuries before Jesus, it had a living tradition since it was read and reread each year, especially during the feast of the Passover. As it was read, people thought of love between man and woman, and their thoughts went back and forth to God's love for his bride Israel. God's love reminded them of such human love, and such human love reminded them of God.

In the Song of Songs we see hints of woman's closeness to earth, and her initiative in drawing man into the great mysteries of sexuality, fertility and love. The bride has the largest part to play in the Song of Songs. There are hints of the woman's primacy in the area of arts, dance and music. The dancing bride is watched by the bridal company, and it is interesting to note how they compare her body to the land and its fertility. They also note her closeness to all of creation by comparing her to various animals, in describing her beauty. The choir sings,

> Your navel is a rounded bowl
> that never lacks mixed wine.
> Your belly is a heap of wheat encircled with lilies.
> Your two breasts are like two fawns,
> twins of a gazelle. . . .
> Your neck is like a tower of ivory
> Your eyes are pools in Heshbon
> by the gate of Bath-rabbim (7:2-4).

In the Song of Songs several of the love poems end with a description of their union in these terms:

> O that his left hand were under my head
> and that his right hand embraced me.
> I adjure you, O daughters of Jerusalem,
> by the gazelles or the hinds of the field,
> That you stir not up, nor awaken love
> until it please (2:6; 8:3).

In other words, the marriage or lovers' union takes place in the outdoors' setting where they are with the animals and all creation who are asked not to disturb them. This pastoral picture brings out the beautiful oneness with all of nature and the universe that is the special contribution of the woman's sexuality.

7. MARY MAGDALENE — THE FIRST ENCOUNTER

Who Was She?

There is an element of mystery right from the beginning in the identity of this woman. As we have seen, women were usually identified in relation to their husband, father or children. Other women in the gospels are identified in this manner. Another Mary is called the mother of Jacob and Joseph (Matthew 27:56). A third Mary is simply Mary of Clopas, meaning most probably the wife of Clopas. But our Mary is simply called "Of Magdala" or the "one called the Magdalene" to indicate that she came from the town of Magdala located on the west coast of the Sea of Galilee, about half way up the lake from its southern outlet into the Jordan River. The name of the town had its origin in the Hebrew word Migdal, meaning tower and the Talmud calls it Migdal Nunya, or "fish tower." Perhaps there once stood a tower erected there as an outlook to observe fishermen at great distances on the lake. Magdala was less than two miles north of the new city of Tiberias which Herod Antipas constructed in 25 A.D. as his capital, and where he erected his palace and government buildings.

If Mary Magdalene was not married, the burning question for any one at the time would be "why not?" We have already seen that woman's place in society was sharply defined by her relationship either to husband, father or children. If women were unmarried, it was usually because of some physical impediment or infirmity that made it impossible for them to marry. This would be very embarrassing for them in the family-oriented society of the time. Luke's gospel hints that Mary was a woman of independent means. He names her first among a group of women who followed Jesus on his journeys and ministered to him *out of their own means* (8:3). This would accord with Mark and Matthew who describe Mary Magdalene at the foot of the cross as first among a group of women who followed him from Galilee ministering to him (Mark 15:40-41; Matthew 27:55-56). Although Jesus and the twelve relied on the hospitality during their journeys, there must have been times when they needed financial support in view of their numbers and the distances they traveled.

What was her occupation? If she were of independent means, where did she get her money? It is quite possible she was an only daughter, and thus received an inheritance when her parents died. There were no "careers" opened for women in those days. Single women at times did run inns or houses of hospitality, but when they did they were often called prostitutes — with or without reason. In the Old Testament, Rahab, the woman who offered hospitality to the twelve spies sent by Joshua before the invasion of Canaan is called a harlot, but is named an innkeeper in the Targum (Aramaic translation) of Joshua 2:1, and by the Jewish historian Josephus. In Roman times, the two occupations often went together. At any rate we can be sure that the mystery and doubt surrounding Mary Magdalene would be enough in her time to earn the epithet "sinner." Mary lived near Tiberius, the luxurious capital city of Herod, where a large number of Gentiles lived. This would certainly have been a source of temptation for her, as well as for men looking for an unattached woman.

First Encounter With Jesus

The gospels do not give us the newspaper-like details that the modern reader would like so much to have. Gospels mean "good news" about the great events of the life, death and resurrection of Jesus. Consequently, these documents put everything else in perspective by placing a veil of anonymity over the many people who came in contact with Jesus. The gospels pass over details that do not bring out the central message.

Mary Magdalene seems to have been a long-time disciple of Jesus, for she followed him from Galilee and stayed with him to the end. She was first of all his disciple and follower. Luke adds another detail that may provide a clue: she was a woman who had been healed of some kind of serious infirmity, which he describes as the result of a possession of seven devils!

> The twelve were with him, and also some women who had been healed of evil spirits and infirmities; Mary, called Magdalene, from whom seven demons had gone out . . . (8:2).

Many ailments, especially those of a nervous nature were connected with the activity of evil spirits; this is why Luke places "evil spirits and infirmities" together. Mary's infirmity must have been a serious one for Luke to mention the number seven, which implies a certain fullness, or completion, or just about the ultimate.

In the gospels there is only one description in detail of a woman's sickness, one that could be really termed a desperate case. This is the cure of the woman with the flow of blood, which is told in great detail in Mark 5:21-34. Mary Magdalene has often been connected with this story, although we cannot be sure. At any rate, the story is meant to typify elements that would go into the healing of a woman. Consequently, Mary Magdalene would certainly have identified herself with this woman, if it were not actually her.

> And there was a woman who had had a flow of blood
> for twelve years, and who had suffered much under
> many physicians, and had spent all that she had,
> and was no better but rather grew worse (5:25).

Such an ailment was the most serious that could affect a
woman. We have already seen that all women were ritually
"unclean" each month for seven days due to the flow of blood.
This was such a powerful "uncleanness" that others could
"catch" it by touching the person, or even by their chance touching her furniture, dishes, clothes, etc. (Leviticus 15:19-24). However, if the flow of blood continued beyond its time, was irregular
or intermittent, the case was regarded as most severe:

> When a woman is afflicted with a flow of blood for
> several days outside her menstrual period, or when
> her flow continues beyond the ordinary period, as
> long as she suffers this unclean flow she shall be
> unclean, just as during her menstrual period
> (Leviticus 15:25-26).

Any cure of such an ailment had to be certified by waiting
seven days after all flow of blood had stopped and then going
to the temple to offer sacrifices as a public witness and atone-
ment for the sin that presumably was the cause of such a
terrible affliction (15:28-30).

We can see now the desperate situation of the woman in the
gospel. She was perpetually unclean. She could never go to the
temple, synagogue or to religious or social gatherings. She was
literally "untouchable." She could touch no one without giving
them her contagion, nor could she be touched. She felt cold and
isolated from the world. Marriage was absolutely out of the
question, for intercourse under such circumstances, as we have

seen, was severely prohibited with hints even of possible death to the transgressor. Such a situation could explain the isolation and independence of Mary. The text also notes how much *she* (not mentioning a husband or father) had spent on physicians, which would only be possible for a woman of means.

> She had heard the reports about Jesus, and came up behind him in the crowd and touched his garment. For she said, "If I touch even his garments I shall be made well" (Mark 5:28).

The story, as told by Mark, is intended to be a teaching on faith, a basic lesson for any disciple, especially Mary as a woman. The first step in faith is the realization of an impossible, incurable situation and the awareness that all human resources are not enough — in this case all the physicians and cures. The second step is hearing about Jesus and approaching him with complete trust in God that the impossible can and will happen. Faith is this basic openness and surrender to God. It is an openness of the entire being, an inner obedience and giving of one's self to God. Openness and surrender might be described as the "feminine side" of human nature of which woman is the symbol. With this trust she approaches him and even touches his garments. This is a daring move because under no conditions was she to touch anyone, for under the Law this would communicate her uncleanness, and in this case make Jesus as unclean as she was.

> And immediately the hemorrhage ceased; and she felt in her body that she was healed of her disease (5:29).

No, she did not give her contagion to Jesus, but touching him was contagious to her: he was above all uncleanness and could share his inner powers to make her whole. In Jesus' contacts with women, they were to learn that the burdensome laws separating them from the world were no longer a barrier. They could talk to him and touch him as freely as sisters in his own home. Mary as a woman thus learned how Jesus' teaching would affect those of her sex.

> And Jesus, perceiving in himself that power had gone forth from him, immediately turned about in the crowd and said, "Who touched my garments?" And his disciples said to him, "You see the crowd pressing around you, and yet you say, 'Who touched me?' " And he looked around to see who had done it (5:30-32).

Here Mark conveys another important lesson about faith that Mary received with her whole heart. Jesus was not a healer-magician. It was only faith on the part of the believer that drew out his powers like a magnet attracts steel. Mary knew that, as a woman, her nature destined her to draw out of a man his deeper powers. Now she saw that there was a deeper level that she could reach, one that everyone could share in, especially women of faith.

> But the woman, knowing what had been done to her, came in fear and trembling and fell down before him, and told him the whole truth (5:33).

In ancient times, all cures were considered part of a turning of the total person to God; it was a religious conversion as well. Sicknesses were psychosomatic in the deepest sense of the word. It was important, then, that she came out publicly before the crowd and testified about what had happened to her. She did so on her knees, in an attitude of prayer and humble submission to God. Mary knew from this moment on that her life would be entirely different. Her independent style of living with its many temptations and not a few lapses was no longer possible. She made the decision to be a follower of Jesus. She would learn from him in the way people learned from a teacher in those days: watching how he acted and imitating it. This meant she would have to stay in his company as much as possible. She would first of all be a disciple, but she did not renounce the traditional role of women in the caring, personal relations within the family. Henceforth she would be part of the new family of Jesus, a family of which Jesus had said, "Whoever does the will of God is my brother and sister and mother to me" (Mark 3:35).

Luke has a story about this transition from the life of a woman "sinner" to a disciple that has, once again, been traditionally associated with Mary Magdalene. Even if it were not so in actual fact, it certainly typifies what went on in her at this time. It illustrates how she would respond to her encounter with Jesus and his complete acceptance of her despite her desperate condition. At any rate, Mary felt her heart simply overflowing with gratitude at the cure she had experienced in the depth of her being. There was a new spark in her whole existence that she could not find words to describe. At the same time she felt a burning love in her heart that simply could not be contained. She knew this was due to the forgiveness and acceptance that Jesus had extended to her during a condition when no other human being would dare touch her, or even come near her. She knew she had to express her affection in some way. In what way could she do this? In the family of Jesus, there were the traditional signs of affection that men and women felt free to exchange. This in itself was a great liberation. She recalled that the woman in the Song of Songs felt a special frustration because she could not express her affection to her lover in public. It simply was not done. Wistfully, the woman desired people to think that he was a brother so that if they kissed, no one would give attention to it as an ordinary family sign of affection. She said,

> Oh, that you were like a brother to me that nursed
> at my mother's breasts! If I met you outside, I would

kiss you and none would despise me. I would lead
you and bring you in to the house of my mother.
There you would teach me to give you spiced wine
to drink, and pomegranate juice (Song of Songs 8:1-
2).

We note in the text that she could be free with him in her
own mother's home, and attend to him, as a brother, preparing
his cup just as her mother prepared the cup of her husband.

In the new family, Jesus showed to his disciples the traditional signs of affection, the embrace and kiss. While these
were usually formalized and brief, Mary did feel an inner and
deep communion at these times. But it was important for her
to give some unusual sign of her affection that would always
be in his memory and hers. For women in the family, there
were two other ways of showing care and affection, and that
was through the washing of feet, and anointing with oil. Mary
carefully prepared herself for a dramatic occasion, which she
felt should be public. She searched through the marketplace
to buy an alabaster jar of very costly perfumed oil, and then
waited for an occasion to use it to anoint Jesus as a sign of her
very special love and gratitude. Luke tells the story in this way,

One of the Pharisees asked him to eat with him, and
he went into the Pharisee's house, and sat at table.
And behold, a woman of the city, who was a sinner,
when she learned that he was sitting at table in the
Pharisee's house brought an alabaster flask of ointment, and standing behind him at his feet, weeping,
she began to wet his feet with her tears, and wiped
them with the hair of her head, and kissed his feet
and anointed them with the ointment (7:36-38).

Mary was actually performing the usual washing of feet by
women that was an ordinary sign of hospitality that the
Pharisee had not shown to Jesus. He had not kissed Jesus as
a sign of welcome and hospitality (7:44-45). Mary did not need

water for the washing; her tears were overabundant and a more personal sign from deep within, for the eyes often reflect deep feeling. No towel was needed, for her long hair, her most precious sign of her womanhood was much better, for it was her very self. Usually anointings were done with ordinary oils, but this oil was purchased at a great price not only of money but of self giving. Anointings were usually done on the head, but this anointing was an especially intimate one of Jesus' feet and thus an extraordinary sign of affection.

All of this, of course, was not lost on the Pharisee, who kept a long distance from anyone with the reputation of a sinner. He wondered if Jesus knew who she was, and if he did know — so much the worse. Jesus could read the thoughts written all over his astonished face. By way of teaching, he told this parable to his host Simon:

> A certain creditor had two debtors; one owed five hundred denarii, the other fifty. When they could not pay he forgave them both. Now which of them will love him more? Simon answered, "The one, I suppose, to whom he forgave more" (7:41-43).

The little parable is meant to bring out the meaning of forgiveness. Those who have received it respond with love and affection. This is because forgiveness is an outpouring of God's love. Those who experience it show love and forgiveness in turn to others. Simon as a "just" man had never really felt the need of forgiveness. This was shown in his attitude both to Jesus and the "sinful" woman. Jesus then said,

> "Do you see this woman? I entered your house, you gave me no water for my feet, but she has wet my feet with her tears and wiped them with her hair. You gave me no kiss, but from the time I came in she has not ceased to kiss my feet. You did not anoint my head with oil but she has anointed my feet with

ointment. Therefore I tell you, her sins, which are many are forgiven, for she loved much; but he who is forgiven little, loves little" (7:44-47).

The expression, "her sins are forgiven, for she loved much" means that her great love is a sign that her sins have been forgiven her. Jesus then affirmed this publicly by saying to her, "Your sins are forgiven." By making this open declaration, Jesus was in effect proclaiming the coming of the Kingdom of God right in his own ministry. For one of the great signs of the coming last days was the open and full forgiveness of sins by God. The prophet Zechariah had written of this day in these words: "On that day there shall be open to the house of David, and to the inhabitants of Jerusalem, a fountain to purify from sin and uncleanness" (13:1). We can understand, then, the reaction of those who were at table with Simon:

Then those who were at table with him began to say among themselves, "Who is this, who even forgives sins?" (7:49)

From this incident and others like it, Mary Magdalene learned the essential meaning of the kingdom of God that Jesus was proclaiming. It was deep and interior, the work of the Spirit of God. At the same time it was external and visible because Jesus so openly accepted and welcomed tax collectors, sinners, outcasts, and even the proud Pharisee. This forgiving and loving acceptance was a great sign of the kingdom of God and the coming last days awaited by every Jew.

Luke's story ends with these words, "And he said to the woman, 'your faith has saved you; go in peace' " (7:50). Shalom (peace) was the ordinary greeting and farewell of these days. But Jesus meant it in the deep, interior sense that Mary experienced. It was the peace of forgiveness, acceptance and love that was the very inner nature of the kingdom of God. Jesus' mission was to bring this peace to the world.

8. IMPRESSIONS OF A WOMAN DISCIPLE

Women in the New Age

Our special interest is to highlight Jesus' ministry and influence from a woman's viewpoint. We have seen in Chapter 6 that women had a subordinate place in what was really a man's world. Typical of this was every Sabbath in the synagogue when the men prayed (and women listened silently) and recited the following blessings, "Blessed be thou, O Lord our God, King of the Universe, who has not made me a Gentile . . . who has not made me a slave, and . . . *who has not made me a woman.*" Centuries later, when women started to pray aloud with the men, the women said instead, "who has created me according to his will."

However, in the New Age, a deep awareness of the Spirit would bring about a true equality for both men and women as equal possessors of the Spirit — which made both sexes alike and equal in their deepest roots. Centuries before, the prophet Joel had hinted at this when he wrote, "Afterwards I will pour my spirit upon all flesh. Your *sons and daughters* will prophesy"

(3:1). Both sexes are mentioned here, and then repeated for emphasis in the next verse where both men servants and female servants are mentioned. The Spirit would be the great equalizer between sexes as well as between social classes.

Already John the Baptist had taken an extraordinary step for his day: he had welcomed women who had come to him at the Jordan for baptism (Matthew 21:31-32). Yet we have noted that only men remained at John's side by the Jordan. Jesus was to go much further than John. He would actually have women disciples with him. This was contrary to all custom, since none of the rabbis of his day would accept female disciples. These women would not play a secondary role but would be regarded as sisters within his own new family (Mark 3:31-35). In regard to women, the Gospel of Thomas preserves a saying of Jesus to the effect that the kingdom will come only when male and female become one. Jesus said this after noting that children were like those who would be entering the kingdom. The disciples asked him, "Shall we then, as children, enter the Kingdom?" Jesus replied,

> When you make the two one, and when you make the inside like the outside and the outside like the inside, and the above like the below, and when you make the male and the female one and the same, so that the male not be male and the female female . . . then will you enter the kingdom (*NHL* II, 37:21-35).

Jesus' teachings on women and their equality as *persons* was not merely theoretic or idealistic. He applied it specifically to the area where women felt it most: marriage laws. We have seen that men were able to divorce their wives as a property procedure. (Women could not divorce men.) They were part of his household, of which he could dispose freely. We can understand then the crucial question addressed to Jesus in Mark 10:2, where the Pharisees came up to test him and asked, "Is it lawful for a man to divorce his wife?" The question in their minds was about how serious a reason was required in view of conflicting schools of opinion about this. They were not challenging the practice itself.

However, in answer, Jesus dismissed the entire matter from consideration. Men cannot divorce women for *any* reason, in view of property rights. She is to be treated as a person, with whom covenants are made. So for this reason Jesus, as beginning the New Age, wishes to restore conditions to their very origins, before the sin and fall of man. So he answers,

> From the beginning of creation, "God made them male and female." For this reason a man shall leave his father and mother and be joined to his wife, and the two shall become one. So they are no longer two but one. What therefore God has joined, let not man put asunder (Mark 10:6-9).

The words here "be joined to a wife" or "cling to a wife" are covenant words used of persons with one another, or persons with God. No man-made property laws can change this.

Jesus as Founder of a Peace Movement

Women are the most serious casualties of war, the ones who suffer the most as their young sons or husbands go off willingly to fight those whom they consider as enemies both of God and their country. Jesus felt a special urgency to begin a national apostolate in view of the increasing underground military movement in Israel and the popular support it was receiving. From his baptismal insight Jesus felt deeply that all, even the non-Jewish world (called the Gentiles, or peoples) were called to a full sharing of the Spirit, and hence complete equality. Had not the prophet Joel said that the Spirit would come upon *all* flesh breaking down class, sex and racial distinctions? In addition, the Spirit in the form of a dove, not a hawk or vulture was a sign of love, peace and reconciliation. It was a Spirit of acceptance and forgiveness.

In view of the unpopularity of a peace movement, Jesus had to take stands that would cause him to lose popular support. Israel was under the control of a cruel foreign oppressor — Roman power and authority. In the American revolutionary war, the Tory was a hated figure in the eyes of an American patriot. Traitor would be too kind a word. Yet many Tories simply did not think that the best way to deal with their English relatives — sometimes even brothers or sisters — was through violence. Many Tories even fled to Canada in order to avoid this. They became an important part of an English-speaking population that would later welcome American conscientious objectors who did not feel they wished to fight in Korea, Vietnam and other places. In Israel the situation was much more acute. The Romans were foreigners, strangers, racially distinct and even worshipers of false gods. Most people quickly put things together and considered a war against Romans as a holy war in which God himself would fight for his people.

Jesus did not fear to take an unpopular stand in this matter, a stand like that of Jeremiah who had warned Israel not to fight the Babylonians before 587 B.C., with the hope that God would fight for them. Most people expected Jesus as a popular prophet to proclaim that God would destroy Rome. Instead he was making strong statements to the effect the temple itself would be destroyed if the people did not change. This was almost political suicide. If a popular preacher exclaims today that God will intervene and destroy Moscow and the "godless" Russians, he will receive few phone calls. But if he or she should say "If this country keeps on going this way the White House will be destroyed" this hints of treason and a threat to the government that might bring an FBI or Secret Service investigation and even arrest. For Jesus, Rome was an oppressor, yes, but it was more important for the people to take responsibility for their own lives and find the oppressor within themselves.

Jesus' reasoning was very simple: If the Spirit made us brothers and sisters equally, even Gentiles, under what conditions could we have the heart to kill a brother or sister? Jesus carried out his peace initiative in very visible and concrete ways that made his message clear to everyone. He took the daring and unpopular initiative to call a despised tax collector, the worst of all Roman puppets, to be a disciple in his intimate family circle. This was a visible sign to everyone about how he felt. There were other things, too, that were especially infuriating to the local people about Roman procedures. Roman soldiers had the custom of forcing civilians to build roads for them. They also requisitioned men to carry heavy loads of food and provisions on their backs under the hot burning sun of Israel. Most people reacted to this with terrible curses. Jesus however said, "If any one forces you to go one mile, go with him two miles" (Matthew 5:41). Imagine a Roman soldier, expecting a curse, who would see a person smile and actually offer to help out another mile with love in his heart!

Jesus taught that the only weapon to fight the Romans or any other enemy was love and nonviolence. The Holy Spirit was a spirit of love, and this was the source of all effective action. And so Jesus could say, in regard to those who suffer from oppression or persecution, "Do not resist one who is evil. But if any one strikes you on the right cheek, turn to him the other also" (Matthew 5:39). When Jesus said, "Love your enemies and pray for those who persecute you," he was not proclaiming a theory but a way of life. He was not talking about mere passive acceptance but about positive action. He described nonviolent action that would "repay" violence by love and even prayer for the well-being of oppressors. Jesus' whole approach was inner-centered, based on the Spirit and love. Only in this way could people be like God. For did not even nature itself mirror the unconditional love of God for everyone, even the sinners and unjust? In asking people to love their enemies and even pray for them, the supreme model was God:

> that you may be sons of your Father who is in heaven;
> for he makes his sun rise on the evil and on the good,
> and sends rain on the just and the unjust (Matthew
> 5:5-46).

Jesus' Secret of Personal Growth: Faith Means Laughter!

For Jesus faith was *ridiculous* in the primary meaning of the word from the Latin *ridere,* to laugh. God's ways are so different from human ways that it is a matter of laughter. In fact one of God's names in Scripture is *He who laughs.* This is found in Psalm 2:4 as God looks upon earth, observing the vain efforts of men to try to overcome his design by their own powers. When Abraham was told by God that he would have a son in his extreme old age, he laughed and laughed (Genesis 17:17). And so did his wife Sarah laugh when she heard the news because she knew she was far beyond the age when it was physically possible for a woman to bear a child (18:12). So when a child did come as a great surprise, Abraham called his son Isaac, which means "laughter" (21:3). When the child was born his mother exclaimed,

> God has made laughter for me; everyone who hears
> will laugh with me. Who would have told Abraham
> that Sarah would nurse children! Yet I have borne
> him a son in his old age (21:6-7).

We have seen that Jesus' model was to imitate God — here the God of Laughter who breaks human stereotypes of possible/impossible routine and habit to create new patterns that make us stop to laugh. Jesus had a real sense of humor. He saw a real contrast between the serious, formal world of religion and the Law he opposed to the simplicity and joy of a religion of the heart.

In addition he was very conscious of what a "man's world" meant in reality. There was a real conflict and contrast between the inner world of the Spirit and the outer world of the society he lived in. To compensate for trust in this inner world, men (and masculinely oriented women) tend to build up an outer world of "gods" they can trust in. This outer world is not real; it exists in their mind. It is composed of all the models, beliefs and expectations in their imagination that they demand of people and situations. In regard to personal security, it was (and is) usual to compensate for inner lack of security by money and possessions. To travel without money in a purse or wallet is ridiculous. Only a fool would do this. Yet Jesus said to his disciples, when they went off to preach, that they were "to take nothing for their journey except a staff; no bread, no bag, no money in their belts" (Mark 6:8-9). Jesus himself did not carry a purse. For the sake of convenience, one of the twelve, Judas, carried a common purse with which he took care of their needs and also those of the poor with anything that remained (John 12:6; 13:28).

In many ways Jesus was like a clown. He knew most people were so stuck and addicted to money that they had to be shocked into seeing things differently. Deliberately putting aside outer security is the only way to really appreciate inner security. The ridiculous behavior was matched by outrageous statements — laughable but true. On being asked if it was possible for a rich man to enter heaven, Jesus replied, "It is easier for a camel to go through the eye of a needle than for a rich man to enter the kingdom of God" (cf. Mark 10:25-27).

In the area of power, Jesus' actions created the most laughter. The everyday world is essentially a world where power and prestige dominate. Competition and getting ahead of others were just as much a part of Jesus' world as ours. The mind-centered individual is constantly thinking of ways of surpassing others, dominating, controlling, or making more money. Many people aspire to be gods, the center of the world and everyone's attention. We leave humble, personal services to others so we can devote our attention to "more important matters." In Jesus' world (and much of today's), these tasks were performed by women.

It is quite unusual to note that Jesus deliberately took occasion to step into the woman's world of personal services. As a clown, he must have delighted in seeing men's shocked faces when he would take food and serve it to them as if he were a woman. Then he would say, "Which is the greater, the one who sits at table, or the one who serves?" (Luke 22:27). Even Mary Magdalene was surprised when he took water and a basin one evening at supper and began to wash the feet of his disciples. This was something she had done many times for others, and especially for Jesus. This was never done by men, except for very important visitors. This task was reserved for women, and in rich households for slaves. Jesus however replied,

> You call me Teacher and Lord; and you are right, for so I am. If I then, your Lord and Teacher, have washed your feet, you also ought to wash one another's feet (John 13:13-14).

The woman's world at his time was the world of children and personal services. For Jesus the most important matter was not only to liberate women, but to *liberate men*! Men needed to enter this inner world of love and service much more than women needed to enter the outer world of men, which was so often a dead-end street. At times when Jesus smiled and laughed, his disciples were keeping in their pent-up anger. After all, the preaching of the kingdom was a serious business, and time should not be wasted. On one startling occasion, a group of women presented their children to Jesus to be blessed. With anger the disciples tried to shoo away the women, rebuking them for taking the Master's time. Jesus however said to them,

> Let the little children come to me, do not hinder
> them; for to such belongs the kingdom of God. Amen
> I say to you, whoever does not receive the kingdom
> of God like a child shall not enter it. And he took
> them in his arms and blessed them, laying his hands
> upon them (Mark 10:13-16).

Jesus' disciples were astonished that they would actually
have to be with children and watch them to learn what the
kingdom was all about. Was not this a woman's role, not a
man's? For Jesus, the child is one who does not know the meaning of the word impossible, one who lives in a world of wonder,
a world not yet encrusted by the filing cabinet world of the
mind where everything becomes ordinary and routine. Jesus
could laugh and play with children, for this is what it is really
all about — spontaneity, living for the moment. The kingdom
of God is right here!

Jesus as trickster had new surprises for his little school each
day. The greatest surprise was the day that a little child made
possible his greatest miracle. Jesus must have laughed each
time he told the story. Like Moses' great miracle of bread in
the desert, Jesus, too, had a mysterious multiplication of loaves
that all started through the intervention of one child. On this
occasion there were some five thousand people with Jesus in
a far-off wilderness place. Sunset was approaching and the
crowds had no provisions for a lengthened stay. The practical-
minded apostles approached the Master and advised him to
send the crowds home so they could purchase food in the towns
and villages. But he said to them, "You yourselves give them
food to eat" (Mark 6:37). The weary apostles must have thought,
"Another one of the Master's great jokes." But they could not
laugh at all. This was an impossible and desperate situation.
So they presented him with the cold logic of business: "Shall
we go and buy two hundred denarii (day's wages) worth of
bread and give it to them to eat?" But Jesus continued on with

his little game (so they thought) and asked, "How many loaves are there? Go and see."

It was only one child in this large crowd who understood Jesus and came up to them with five barley loaves and two fish (John 6:9). These were not supermarket loaves, but the small, flat, pancake type loaves that he kept in a pouch on his belt as a kind of picnic lunch to use on trips and journeys. What a joke! The crowds must have laughed. How absurd it was to bring out this food for so great a multitude. But Jesus knew that the joke was really on them. With a grateful smile he accepted the loaves from the child and began giving them out in a mysterious manner, until everyone had enough to eat. Not only that, but there were actually twelve full baskets left over. Then Jesus began to laugh. The greatest miracle of all had taken place because one child did not know the meaning of the word "impossible" and was willing to share his food in obedience to Jesus' word: "you yourselves give them to eat." This child had taught them how to do away with world hunger: by trusting that there is enough food for everyone if we only begin to share and then let this contagious miracle of sharing spread through the world.

Jesus' sense of humor and his best tricks were reserved for the solemn, religious establishment. The frequent fasting and ascetic lives of some religious leaders made their faces sad and gaunt as they walked along the streets. But Jesus said to his disciples, "When you fast, anoint your heads and wash your faces as everyone will think you are joyfully going to a wedding or party" (cf. Matthew 6:19). In fact, when a friend's wedding occurred, Jesus was there, enjoying the singing, the dancing and abundant flow of wine (John 2:1-11). Jesus' favorite image of God was the wedding feast. This was the greatest event in the lives of the poor country people. Such festivities went on for a full seven days; all work stopped and there was abundant choice food for everyone and fine wine. It was a joyful extraordinary time — in fact the only time when men, women, and children could freely intermingle. Everyone looked forward to seeing the bride unveiled in the wedding procession. But most unusual of all, it was the one time in life when all the positive requirements of the Law were suspended for the bride, groom and wedding party. When Jesus announced often that the kingdom of God was like a wedding feast (Matthew 22:1), he must have smiled with joy for he knew that in the New Age the inner joy of the Spirit would take the place of the external seriousness of religious obligations.

Mary Magdalene always remembered the time when Jesus pulled one of his unforgettable jokes. They were entering the town of Jericho one day and the crowds jammed the roads to catch a glimpse of Jesus. But there was a little man, Zacchaeus, who was not only short in external stature but internally as well, for he was the chief tax collector, literally the worst rascal in Jericho. He ran ahead and climbed up a sycamore tree in order to see Jesus better. A preacher once described Zacchaeus as the first man to go out on a limb for Christ! While the pun is bad, the preacher saw the humor in the situation as Jesus stopped and laughed. He looked up into the tree and said, "Zacchaeus, hurry up and come down. I'm going to have dinner in your house today." This was no joke for the many respectful law-observing folk in the town. They all murmured, for each had hoped the Master would select their house to stay in. But Jesus said to all of them, "Today salvation has come to this house, since he also is a son of Abraham. For the Son of man came to seek and save the lost" (Luke 19:1-10).

While Jesus could be laughing and joyful, he could also be very sad at times, when he saw how slow the twelve were to understand his inner message on the primacy of the Spirit. They could not put power out of their minds. They knew that repentance and inner change came first, but they never dismissed the idea that the time would come for Jesus to openly display his power to become the long-awaited political leader to liberate his people from the Gentiles. Yes, the kingdom would begin within, but it must eventually be an external realm where Jesus would be the leader everyone looked up to. Especially when they moved toward Jerusalem in what looked like a climactic journey, they began to discuss among themselves the various offices, positions of power and roles they would have in that kingdom.

Once again Jesus had to shock them out of their "men's club" world where they discussed such competitive matters. He asked them what they were discussing along the way. But they were silent and embarrassed for they were discussing with one another who would be greatest in the coming great event of the establishment of the kingdom. Once again Jesus called a little child, and stood in the center of the twelve with a little child in his arms and said, "Whoever receives one such child in my name receives me, and whoever receives me receives not me but him who sent me" (Mark 9:36-37). Mary Magdalene let these words sink in deeply, for she knew they could only be understood in the world of women and children where the inconspicuous little services to children as persons were matters reaching to the very heart of the kingdom. Men in their world found it so hard to understand these things because they were simply not involved in them on a regular basis — if at all.

9. THE JERUSALEM CRISIS: MARY AND JUDAS; THE TEST OF FRIENDSHIP

Jesus knew that, as a prophet, he must present a convincing public stand in Jerusalem, the capital city. Jerusalem was the stronghold of official Judaism, the sacred city where the mysterious Ark of God resided in its special temple. God's presence was enthroned above the Ark between the two guardian cherubim — mysterious winged creatures indicating the presence of the deity. Jerusalem was also the political capital where the high priest, appointed by Rome, presided over the ruling Sanhedrin, which was composed of 70 priests and Scribes, many of whom were members of the strict Pharisee party.

Passover was the best time for Jesus to come to Jerusalem, for there would be crowds from all over Israel, and even Jewish visitors from foreign countries. However, it would be a very dangerous time as well. Frequent riots took place on this great feast day of the Jews' liberation from Egypt — the symbol of any foreign power that tried to enslave the Jews. The situation was so tense that extra Roman troops were garrisoned in Jerusalem during the Passover. They were marched in from the governor's headquarters at Caesarea. For Pilate as Roman governor, it was a time of great tension for he had already antagonized Jewish people by his insensitivity to their religious beliefs. Any suspicion of a revolt or disturbance among the people must be promptly squelched by a convincing show of force.

Jesus made careful plans for his entry into Jerusalem. It would be a good opportunity to obtain widespread publicity about who he was and what he was trying to do. The excitement of the people reached a high pitch during the Passover feast-days, and there must be no mistake about his mission of peace. He prepared three dramatic signs, two for the public and one for his disciples. He knew the customary way that powerful military leaders and kings marched up the great hill to the gates of Jerusalem. The Romans always came with a great display of power with their iron chariots and shining steel armor. The kings of Israel in the past often rode to Jerusalem on horses and chariots.

Jesus entered Jerusalem seated upon an ass, along with his company of disciples spreading a triumphant carpet of olive branches and palms along the road before him. For those who witnessed the event and knew the Scriptures, the message was obvious: Jesus' claim to leadership was as Messiah of Peace bringing the message of love and nonviolence even for the ruthless Roman oppressors. The Scripture relating to Jesus was familiar, yet strange and mysterious: that of humble king riding into Jerusalem not on a conquering horse but on a humble ass. He was a leader who had a mission to banish the implements of war and proclaim peace to the world (Zechariah 9:9-10). Jesus took personal charge of the details of his entry, making a clear connection between the Scriptures and his action. The disciples enthusiastically cooperated in the event singing royal acclamations along the route: "Hosanna to the Son of David! Blessed is he who comes in the name of the Lord!" (Matthew 21:9). Jesus' disciples added their own dramatic flair by laying down their cloaks for the donkey to step on, thus providing a royal road to Jerusalem. At first Jesus and his disciples were alone, but gradually more people joined as they understood the meaning behind the event. While people wanted liberation from Rome, only a minority pushed for violent revolution.

When Jesus drew near the city gate and looked at the magnificent temple and the glittering houses of Jerusalem, he came to a halt as a vision of terror came into his mind. For an instant he saw his beloved city besieged by Roman troops and the temple of God being torn down stone by stone. Tears streamed from his eyes. Luke writes,

> And when he drew near and saw the city, he wept over it, saying "Would that even today you knew the things that make for peace! But now they are hidden from your eyes. For the days shall come upon you, when your enemies will cast up a bank around you and surround you, and hem you in on every side . . . (19:39-43).

Suddenly, Jesus realized he would not be successful as a Messiah of Peace. The majority would follow military leaders who would lead a revolution against Rome causing horrible sufferings, the death of thousands of Jews, and the destruction of the temple.

Not wishing to lose momentum, Jesus followed up this procession event on the next day by a solemn entry into the temple area, as a second great messianic sign. Every great leader was expected to enter the temple area in triumph. During the last times in history, God's final intervention on earth, it was prophesied that the Messiah would enter the temple (Malachi 3:1). The popular interpretation of the prophecy was that God would intervene with a mighty act of power to clean out the oppressive Gentiles who were defiling Jerusalem and the temple area (the court of the Gentiles).

By entering and cleansing the temple, Jesus surprised everyone. The prophet Zechariah's final words also spoke of the coming day of the Lord. This prophet had written about the purification of the temple that would really make it a holy place. He had said, "There shall no longer be a trader in the house of the Lord of hosts on that day" (14:21). In the Hebrew text of the prophet, the word for trader is *Canaanite*. However, it also means "foreigner" and the usual explanation was that the text referred to the purification of *foreigners* (Romans) from the temple. Jesus, however, wished to restore the prophecy to its original meaning. He held that inner holiness was primary, and the sign here would be the removal of the traders and business men from the temple.

To make his explanation of the prophecy clear, Jesus dramatized it in action:

> He entered the temple and began to drive out those
> who sold, and those who bought in the temple, and
> he overturned the tables of the money changers and
> the seats of those who sold pigeons (Mark 11:15-16).

In order to make his application concrete and specific, he would not let the merchants carry their goods through the temple area (11:16).

When Jesus had concluded his action, he summed it up with these words,

> Is it not written, "My house shall be called a house
> of prayer for all the nations." But you have made it
> a den of robbers (11:17).

Far from clearing out Gentiles from the temple, Jesus wished to open one temple to everyone.

Jesus' action precipitated a crisis for Jerusalem's political and religious leaders. Jesus had publicly shown his authority in the temple area, which was under their supervision. As members of the Sanhedrin, the Roman puppet government, they would be responsible for any public demonstrations caused by Jesus' actions. Many of them felt obliged to denounce him to Rome as a dangerous leader. Mark simply notes,

> And the chief priests and the Scribes heard it and sought a way to destroy him, for they feared him, because all the multitude was astonished at his teaching (12:18).

When Jesus' disciples noticed the anger and determined reaction of the temple authorities, fear came over them. The master's actions had succeeded in their teaching goals, but what good would result if he failed to overcome the determined opposition? His quick elimination from the scene could come before he had the chance to gather a strong enough popular following. Most of the disciples clung to the hope that Jesus would finally reveal his great power, just as Moses did in liberating his people. Why confront the open power of the Jerusalem establishment with mysterious teachings of peace and love?

Jesus read his disciples' minds. On the next day, he looked across to Jerusalem with his disciples from the nearby Mountain of Olives. Then he told them to accomplish the seemingly impossible: in this case, overcoming the mountain of opposition in Jerusalem. He said,

> Whoever says to this mountain, "Be taken up and cast into the sea" and does not doubt in his heart, but believes that what he says will come to pass, it will be done for him. Therefore I tell you, whatever you ask in prayer, believe that you receive it, and you will (Mark 11:23-24).

The secret is to ask with such confidence, that *you already see what you ask as actually happening* — "Believe that you are receiving it."

Meanwhile, as the feast of Passover drew near, rumors reached the little band that the chief priests and elders were seeking a way to secretly arrest Jesus and have him sentenced before the Passover. This would be necessary to prevent an uprising or riot that might be supported by many Galilean supporters of Jesus who had come up to the feast. The whole atmosphere was tense with danger. While not in Jerusalem, Jesus and his close followers stayed in Bethany a few miles from Jerusalem. There they nervously discussed their plan of action in the atmosphere of growing threats.

Jesus was determined to go ahead with his ministry in the capital. He felt he was a prophet, called to speak openly to his people, as Jeremiah, Isaiah, and others had done in Jerusalem, despite the possibility of death. One of the most trusted and responsible men among the twelve, Judas, was the spokesman for the fears of all the disciples. Very practically he said, "Master, if you are arrested and put to death, that will simply be the end for you and all of us. Where will this kingdom of God be that you are always talking about? Power is needed at this time, not talking and signs. At this time it would be better to withdraw from Jerusalem and consolidate your position with your followers from Galilee and other regions. Then we can face the Jerusalem establishment and force them to listen to us."

Jesus reminded them, as he had on other occasions, that he had an inner source of nourishment and power — his complete openness and obedience to the will of his Father. He recalled to them the time they brought him food and he refused to eat, saying, "My food is to do the will of him who sent me, and to accomplish his work" (John 4:34). To make his meaning about the will of God plainer he made this parallel: "All the earth is simply filled with energy, power and presence of God." Isaiah wrote of this when he described the angels as singing, "All the earth is filled with his glory" (6:3). Whenever a person does the will of God, this divine energy becomes concentrated and centered in that person as a source of divine strength and becomes available for others. Like a great bolt of lightning, it finds a pole or tree and moves through to the ground. In the same way, we ground the divine energy everytime we are completely open to God and obey him. When this is obedience even in the face of death, the results bring divine energy and grace to the whole world.

Although few of the disciples spoke out like Judas, many felt the same way, though they remained silent and bewildered. None of the men spoke out to support the Master while they were all together at Bethany for dinner. However, the gospels tell the detailed story of one woman who took a public stand, not by her words but by her actions and supported what Jesus was going to do. She bought an expensive alabaster jar of ointment of pure nard. Going up to Jesus, she broke the jar and poured all of its precious contents over his head. With her fingers she slowly and lovingly anointed his face and forehead. The disciples, especially Judas, were quick to react. They could not attack the Master, but they attacked her waste and lack of concern for the poor. Jesus himself defended her action. The woman expressed her personal testimony of love and support for his course of action, which might lead to the cross, death and burial. Jesus said,

> Why do you trouble the woman? For she has done a beautiful thing to me. For you always have the poor with you but you will not always have me. In pouring this ointment on my body she has done it to prepare me for burial. Amen, I say to you, wherever this gospel is preached in the whole world, what she has done will be told in memory of her (Matthew 26:10-13).

The woman's name is not given in the gospel story, but she must have been a prominent disciple to be with Jesus at this time. She is also connected with the burial of Jesus, and was publicly announced as a model for others to imitate. What she did is more important than her name, yet Mary Magdalene fits best if we try to identify the woman in the story. Mary Magdalene was the first-named woman and witness at the death and burial of Jesus (Mark 15:40, 47) (for the identification of this woman with Mary of Bethany, in John's gospel, see Chapter 13). Mary Magdalene had the courage to confront Judas and the other male disciples at this crucial point in the life of Jesus.

Judas was simply furious because of the way he had come off before others in a confrontation with Mary Magdalene. He went outside into the night, where the Prince of Darkness had been watching the turn of events. Now was his time, and he worked carefully on Judas; his chief weapon was despair. Giving up hope of winning the Jerusalem leadership, Judas pondered what to do. Since there was no further possibility of saving the Master from disaster, he must think of himself and his country. As a good citizen he should warn the Sanhedrin, and inform them where they could secretly seize Jesus before it was too late. The priests should compensate him for what he would do. So Judas went to the chief priests and discussed the best way he could betray Jesus for arrest in secret without publicity or danger of inciting a riot.

With a very heavy heart Jesus prepared his third great sign for his disciples alone. He knew what Judas was up to, yet what Jesus planned to do involved love, even for his betrayer. This last sign would be a great surprise to all. Two disciples were to walk into Jerusalem and see a strange sight — a man doing a woman's job of carrying water — Jesus' favorite paradox of reversed roles — and follow the man to the house where he was bringing the water. Then they should ask where the guest room for their Passover was to be. The final surprise was to be led to a room furnished and ready for their celebration of the Passover.

In this last sign Jesus began to hand over to his disciples his final and greatest gift of all. At his baptism, Jesus experienced so intimate and complete union with the Spirit that Spirit and self became one. It was like a marriage union, two in one flesh. As time went on, the deep dimensions of this union became more apparent to him. The only way he could explain it was by way of the "heart-transplant" promised by Ezechiel in the New Age when God had said, "A new heart I will give you, and a new spirit I will put within you" (36:26).

Jesus knew the Spirit worked wonders of love in every human heart: The love of mothers and fathers toward their children and vice versa; the love of spouses and good friends toward each other; the love and care for the sick and aged. The spirit in Jesus expanded his love to include the love in every human heart since the creation of the universe. The Spirit, the Creative Word of God made his heart like a great throbbing heart of the Universe. What better gift could he give to his disciples than the secret of his inner being — this new cosmic heart — made possible by the Spirit. Yet his heart was himself, and he was his heart. He would have to give himself completely so they could share all that he had.

The secret sign of Jesus was ordinary and simple — bread and wine. Not by any magic power, but because he wanted it so; his words had power. He desired to be remembered and totally experienced. It was to be the Supper of the Lord — the supper under his command. All human beings need nourishment. When they eat (break bread) they will often remember him especially at solemn times. Bread always did have a depth of meaning. A favorite passage of Jesus was, "Man does not live by bread alone, but by every word that proceeds from the mouth of God" (Deuteronomy 8:3). Behind bread was the creative Word of God, the source of all nourishment. Bread and wine were now to be a means of the deepest possible union between Master and disciple. Divine Wisdom had used this symbolism to describe the union of divine Wisdom with her disciples in these words: "Come eat of my food, and drink of the wine I have mixed" (Proverbs 9:5).

With these thoughts, Jesus sat down with his disciples at their final meal together. He loved them all, even Judas who sat near him. In fact, he showed him special attention and care by offering him choice morsels from the common dish. When the moment for the final sign came, Jesus' actions were deliberate. His disciples felt that something special was about to happen. They had always been aware of the reverence and care with which he broke bread; but now it was more striking than it ever had been.

Jesus took bread and slowly pronounced the traditional blessing over it: "Blessed be thou O Lord our God, King of the universe, who brings forth bread from the earth!" "Yes," he reflected, "Bread is from the earth, and the earth is from the Creator and Sustainer of all. I want to give this earth-bread, the source of all nourishment, to my disciples." Then Jesus reverently broke the bread in pieces and said to them, "Take and eat; this is my body which is for you. Do this in remembrance of me." The disciples lifted their heads in astonishment. Jesus identified the bread with himself. In eating it, they came into a new intimate union and identity with him. Yet they could not possibly grasp all that was deep in the Master's mind. The bread represented his body, his total self, especially the heart, the center of his being which was transfixed by the dove-Spirit. It was the new Spirit, the love-filled heart promised by Ezechiel the prophet. The disciples were to eat it in the deepest possible sense. They were to assimilate not just food, but the inner source of all nourishment. Jesus' life, dominated by the Spirit, was to be their life. His great expansive heart, the cosmic heart of the Universe was to be their heart. This was the real "heart transplant" promised by Ezechiel, Jesus' gift was total and complete; he could give no more.

Later during the meal, Jesus took a cup of wine, and pronounced the usual blessing with these words, "Blessed be thou

O Lord our God who creates the fruit of the vine." Then he said, "This cup is the new covenant in my blood. Do this as often as you drink it in remembrance of me." The sharing of the cup brought out a new element in meaning. To drink from a common cup was a sign of solemn agreement or covenant. Such a sharing was even done (and still is) during a Jewish marriage ceremony as a sign of the vows of the spouses to one another for life. The symbolism of blood engulfed the whole ritual of the cup. Wine was appropriate because it was called in ordinary speech, "the blood of the grape." The grape had to be crushed and die to produce the spirited wine. Jesus was ready to give his life as a prophet. The radical openness and obedience of Jesus to the will of the Father lie behind the whole scene. At this moment, Jesus was determined to go ahead, and so in a sense it was already done. Death itself would be the final seal to show the world the complete identity he had with the Father through their oneness of purpose and will. Only "obedience unto death" would consummate for all eternity his inner marriage with the Holy Spirit.

When Jesus spoke the words, "new covenant of blood," he also had in mind the new heart covenant that was promised by God through the prophet Jeremiah: "The days are coming when I will make a new covenant. . . . I will put my law within them, and I will write it upon their hearts . . ." (31:31-33).

Judas finally could stand it no longer and walked out of the upper room (John 13:30). Most of the others thought little of it. It was customary to give alms to the poor and Judas held the common purse, or perhaps he needed to purchase something needed for the feast (John 13:27). Judas knew where Jesus would spend the night — at his favorite spot on the Mountain of Olives — so he hurried to the Sanhedrin leaders. He gave them the needed information to arrest Jesus secretly and take him away without any disturbance. It was dark outside as well as inside Judas' heart as the Dark Master took control of him. Now Jesus' own supreme test lay immediately ahead of him.

10. THE CROSS, THE COSMIC STRUGGLE AND THE MYSTERY OF THE TWO MARYS

It was late Thursday night when the weary group of disciples left their banquet room in Jerusalem. They walked the short distance down Mount Zion and up the Mount of Olives where they were spending the night outdoors during their stay in Jerusalem. It was a favorite spot of quiet, reflection and prayer for Jesus. The men spread out their rolled up straw mats on the ground in a circle around Jesus. The women also made their own circle a short distance away. Everyone was afraid since Judas had not returned. Peter and the others obtained swords and placed them by their pillows.

Jesus felt that this night would bring decisive action from the Sanhedrin leaders. The Passover feast had begun at sunset; any moves they made must be accomplished quickly, before morning. Jesus reflected on his own predicament and that of his little group. Under cover of darkness, there was still time to move out quickly. By daybreak, they could be well on their way to Galilee where they would be much safer. If he waited, Jesus believed Judas would betray his presence to the temple

police. They would certainly arrest him, bring him to trial and
hand him over to the Roman governor who would sentence him
to the horrible death of the cross. What should he do? Jesus
knew he had to pray for strength to make this greatest decision
of his life. Needing the special support of others at this time,
he asked Peter, James and John, his closest male disciples to
accompany him in prayer. They left the sleeping circle of disciples and went off a short distance to a nearby grove of olive trees.

At this hour the great cosmic struggle began. The Dark Master made his plans carefully. Slowly and steadily, he would
apply pressure until the proper moment came for him to unleash
all his terrible power. Jesus was now in full strength and possession of his powers, but would he be so later? Satan was
aware that everything depended on Jesus' willingness to do his
Father's will. The devil knew the importance of the Creator's
will, the one who had said, "Let there be light and light was
made" (Genesis 1:3). He must get Jesus to bend or compromise
in his resolve.

Jesus began to pray standing with his arms outstretched.
Then he knelt on the ground to make his supplications all the
more intense. A wave of fear came over him as his imagination
pictured the coming events if he stayed in Jerusalem. Satan
used his powers over the human imagination to intensify and
heighten these scenes. One powerful image after another came
into Jesus' mind. First, the condemnation by Pilate; then the
endless cruel scourging by Roman soldiers; and finally the hor-
ror of the cross. The cold sweat of death came upon his forehead.
He said to Peter and the others, "My soul is very sorrowful,
even to death; remain here, and watch" (Mark 14:34).

As Jesus envisioned the sufferings ahead, he fell on the
ground and collapsed. He asked his Father that, if possible,
this terrible prospect be spared him. After all, how would his
death help in the proclamation of the kingdom of God? A con-
tradiction existed: on one hand, he had to live in order to fulfill
his mission as a prophet; yet on the other hand, if he left

Jerusalem, he would be disobedient to his Father's will that he face death in the capital city. For a moment Jesus was bewildered and did not know what to do.

Was there any parallel to his situation in the Scriptures to offer hope? Jesus remembered the great Jewish model of obedience, Isaac, the son of Abraham. Here, too, God had asked the impossible — that Abraham sacrifice his son, and yet this son's continued life was necessary to fulfill God's plan and promises. Jesus recalled the words Isaac said to his father Abraham (who represented God's will). Isaac said (in the Aramaic translation) *Abba* (meaning father) and Abraham had answered, "Yes, son." Isaac continued, "Behold, the fire and the wood, but where is the lamb for the burnt offering?" (Genesis 22:7-8). With these words Isaac went bravely ahead into the unknown, trusting in God and his father Abraham.

With this image in mind, Jesus prayed to his Father in the same way that Isaac had spoken to his human father. He used the intimate family term, *Abba*. It was the expression of a dedicated, obedient son, ready to go ahead and obey the will of God no matter what it might cost. Jesus said, "Abba, Father, all things are possible to you; remove this cup from me; yet not what I will, but what you will" (Mark 14:36).

About an hour later, Jesus came back to where Peter, James and John had been praying. They were fast asleep. Saddened and wearied, Jesus woke them up and begged them to pray with him, saying, "Watch and pray that you do not enter into temptation; the spirit indeed is willing but the flesh is weak" (14:38). Again Jesus returned to prayer and kept repeating the same words — "Abba, Father" and "thy will be done," but he could feel no answer to prayer.

Once again he came back to the three disciples only to find them sleeping once more. A wave of despair and discouragement came over him, yet he returned to prayer. The sleeping disciples already hinted at the future; all of them would desert him, and some even deny him. He could not count on them. Judas his close friend, whom he had trusted so much, had already betrayed him. What use was it to go on if no one continued his work? There appeared no alternative but to immediately wake up the disciples and get out fast. Judas was probably on his way with soldiers at this very moment.

Over in the women's circle, Mary Magdalene could not sleep. She knew what an agonizing night of decision Jesus faced. In her own mind, she could imagine Jesus' thoughts. It was not a night for sleep but for watching and prayer. From the distance, Mary saw Jesus and the three go off to pray. Quietly, she, too, arose, placed her knees on her straw mat and raised her arms in prayer. She would stand by Jesus this night no matter what it might cost her in physical effort.

Jesus knew he must make a decision soon. Due to lack of sleep, his head nodded in exhaustion. He then noticed Mary Magdalene praying in the distance. With her arms outstretched in the moonlight she looked like her name, *magdal* — a tower. Jesus knew that he was not alone. He took a deep breath and experienced once more the power of the Spirit/Breath of God within him. Jesus was confident that not only Mary Magdalene, but another Mary, his mother, supported him now in his hour of need. Jesus made his decision: he would not wait for Judas to arrest him but walk out to meet him.

The rattling of armor, and the glow of torches in the distance warned Jesus that his enemies were approaching. Judas had agreed with the priests on a secret sign to identify the Master in the dark so an arrest could be made quietly and quickly. Judas would go up and kiss the Master — something he had often done as a member of Jesus' family circle. This kiss was the cruelest blow Jesus had ever received in his life. He shuddered as Judas' face touched his. Mary Magdalene was shocked and could identify with Jesus' feelings.

The little band was ready for armed resistance. Peter quickly drew his sword and wounded one of the armed servants of the high priest. Jesus ordered them to put back their swords and not resist. His mission was of love, peace and nonviolence. He would be faithful to this despite the possibility that resistance might offer the opportunity to escape in the dark. The soldiers arrested Jesus and bound him securely. At this point all Jesus' disciples left him and fled (Mark 14:50).

The male disciples of Jesus were in special danger. Any identification of them would surely lead to their arrest and their crucifixion with Jesus. Women were in less danger and could follow the ensuing events from a distance. They could not enter the courtyard of the high priest where Jesus was immediately conducted. Soon afterward, Mary Magdalene was shocked when Peter came out in tears and told the disciples he had three times denied even knowing the Master.

The informal night trial of Jesus before the Jewish council was swiftly convened. Jesus' peace statements were twisted into an accusation that he intended to destroy God's temple, and this of course was blasphemous. Jesus had indeed predicted that the temple would be destroyed if the nation did not receive a Messiah of peace but trusted in military leaders. Yet this was meant to be a warning, a conditional prophecy. The high priest and council decided to hand over Jesus to Pilate for judgment. The charge would be the only one that interested the Romans: that this Jesus claimed to be king of the Jews. The Sanhedrin as the official puppet government was obliged to present such pretenders to Roman authority, and they knew Rome would not hesitate to eliminate anyone who threatened their rule. Caesar alone was emperor and king.

Jesus was imprisoned until morning, guarded by temple soldiers. From the outside, Mary Magdalene and the women could hear the rough game these soldiers played (Luke 22:63-64). It was called, "playing the prophet" and of course Jesus was a most suitable victim. It consisted in blindfolding the "prophet" and then giving him a blow on the cheeks or a spit on the face. Then the "prophet" would be asked to identify who it was that struck him. In ordinary games, if the name was guessed, the identified person would change places and become the prophet. In the case of Jesus, who gave no answer, this was not possible.

At daybreak, Jesus was secretly conducted to the pretorium of Pilate. There must be no opportunity for a public disturbance. The high priests gathered together a small crowd of their loyal supporters to stand outside the pretorium to put pressure on Pilate for a quick sentence. In the gospels, Pilate appears vacillating and unwilling to sentence Jesus. However, history indicates he was a cruel and ruthless governor. In fact, Rome finally had to remove him from office because he was unbearable to the Jewish people. It did not take long to convince Pilate that Jesus was a messianic pretender who might possibly instigate a rebellion. The death sentence was quickly obtained, and Pilate wrote the official reason for his execution on a parchment to be placed over Jesus' head on the cross. The inscription read, "the king of the Jews."

Since Jesus' male disciples had all fled at his arrest, it was only the women who could follow the events at a distance. They obtained some news by hearsay, and guessed at other things from what they could hear outside the pretorium of Pilate. When Pilate came out before the crowd, they heard the high priest's henchmen screaming, "Crucify him, crucify him." After the death sentence, the women knew that the Romans usually scourged prisoners before the crucifixion, but from outside they could only hear the blows.

Jewish scourgings were mercifully limited to thirty-nine blows, one short of the legal limit of forty. They were meant as a warning and a punishment. Roman scourgings were merciless and unlimited, meant to weaken prisoners so they would quickly die on the cross. Often the scourging alone resulted in death. The scourging of revolutionaries was done with a special vengeance, since the Romans knew these persons made them risk their lives in battle and sometimes even killed their comrades.

It was a pitiful sight when the soldiers finally brought out Jesus and began to conduct him to the place of execution. With Jesus there were two others who had instigated riots. For the Romans, Jesus was simply one of many who met the same fate. The Roman governor hoped that frequent executions would stop the revolutionary fever among the Jews. The soldiers placed the heavy wooden cross on Jesus' shoulders and pushed him along the way. They had to pull him to his feet several times when he stumbled or fell exhausted. Finally, when Jesus had no strength to go further, the soldiers forced an African from the Roman province of Cyrene to carry the cross for him. Jesus was completely alone. His only friends present were Mary Magdalene and a few women who were not permitted too close to him but could only follow from a distance.

When the procession of condemned men reached Golgotha, it was about Friday noon. Golgotha was called the "skull place" because so many executions took place on that spot. A slightly elevated location at the intersection of important roads to Jerusalem, it was a good place for the Romans to make a public example of those who dared defy their authority. Crucifixions were routine for them, but it is hard to imagine the excruciating pains and horrible screams of agony. The iron hammers pushed the long nails though muscles, flesh and tendons. People who witnessed executions were often tormented by their images for the rest of their life. For Mary and the others, each blow struck into their own hearts as they shared Jesus' agony. The Romans went about their work with precision, hoisting up the crosses with ropes and pulleys. They stripped their prisoners of their clothes to shame them publicly. Then they methodically divided among themselves any possessions of the condemned by drawing lots.

As a token of mercy, the Roman soldiers usually allowed a drugged drink to be given to their victims. The gospels note that Jesus refused to take it (Mark 15:22-23). Jesus intended to be fully alert right until the end. Under the hot sun, due to rapid loss of blood and dehydration, Jesus' strength steadily failed. The sun moved down the horizon toward sunset and black clouds of rain gathered overhead. It was Jesus' darkest hour and he gave himself to prayer. He used Psalm 22, the prayer of the innocent suffering servant of God. Jesus' first words were distinctly audible: "My God, my God, why have you forsaken me" (Mark 15:34). Jesus could continue no further for his parched tongue stuck to his throat.

From a distance, Mary Magdalene and her companions sensed the final moments were near. They stretched their arms to heaven in intense prayer. Mary Magdalene turned her eyes to Jesus on the cross. She focused all her energy in that gaze, trusting it would bring him help in this desperate hour.

Meanwhile the Prince of Darkness had been waiting for the moment when Jesus' energies were so depleted that he could no longer resist his temptations. The black gathering clouds took on an ominous symbolism, and the whole atmosphere was filled with tension. During all human history the Dark Master had never needed to use his full powers. He usually won easy victories over men and women conditioned by dreams of power, money and security. All he needed to do was to slightly enhance these dreams and people would act as willing pawns to do his wishes. Now, however, Satan turned his gaze toward the cross, concentrating his full power. Never since creation had the universe witnessed so irresistible a force.

Far away in Galilee, on Friday morning, news reached Jesus' mother and family about the crisis in Jerusalem. They heard about Jesus' encounter with the priests in the temple and feared for the worst. They had not gone to this Passover because of the dangers involved to themselves as well as to Jesus. Mary had been in silent communion with her son for the last few days, sending him energy through prayer at a time when she knew he really needed it. No time was left for her to journey to Jerusalem and be at his side. Now on this Friday, his mother felt once more the movement of the sword in her heart that she experienced the first time Jesus returned to Galilee with the news of his mission. The sounds and blows of an approaching crucifixion already echoed in her heart. She wondered what a poor woman like herself could do at such a distance. (The mention of Jesus' mother by the cross in John 19:25 is not found in the other gospels, and perhaps refers to her presence as a remembering mother and associate.)

Mary thought of Jesus' favorite place of prayer, the mountain where he often withdrew for solitude and strength. She left Nazareth and walked across the plain to Mt. Tabor, some six miles away. Then she made the slow and exhausting climb to the summit, some 1000 feet above the valley. As she made the ascent, more than once she was tempted by despair — what good was it all at this point? Her mind searched for Scriptures for a model and example. She remembered the story in the book of Judith. There, one woman prayed, trusted in God's will and single-handedly won a victory over the Persian General Holofernes. The name Judith meant "the Jewess," for she summed up the best qualities of the Jewish people. Mary thought, "Yes, that is who I am. I am Mary-Judith. I am not here alone, but together with me are the hopes and aspirations of all my people."

When Mary reached the summit, the sun was already moving toward the horizon. In the distant south, she could see the hills of Judea where Jerusalem was located. Black storm clouds were gathering over the city. She sensed the power of the Prince of Darkness in those black clouds. Mary could feel that this was a cosmic struggle between Jesus and Satan, the ruler of this world. She shuddered at the thought. What could she possibly do against the wily Serpent who had never been defeated, least of all by a woman? Was there any hope in this darkest hour of history when Jesus' forces were at their last ebb? Did the Scriptures contain anything about the birth of the New Age that could provide hope?

The image came to her of the Serpent in the Garden of Eden and his encounter with the Woman, the Mother of all the living. The Serpent had attacked and defeated the Woman, giving her a terrible wound. However, God said in the Scriptures that the Woman and her offspring would finally crush the Serpent's head in victory. God said to the Serpent,

> I will put enmity between you and the woman
> and between your seed and her seed;
> He will bruise your head,
> And you shall bruise his heel. (Genesis 3:15)

With this new confidence, and a fresh burst of energy, Mary turned toward Jerusalem. The setting sun shone around her garments, and the Passover moon was at her back; the twelve tribes of Judah were the crown about her head. She felt transformed into the eternal Woman who makes it possible for man to be lifted up and freed from the clutches of darkness. With her knees in the soft ground, Mary was one with mother earth. She was ready to wrestle with the Prince of Darkness for her son. God had opened her womb to give her this unusual son; forty days after his birth, she had presented him as a priest to God (Luke 2:22-24) and she had never taken back her offering. She would see him through the darkest moment of his life, lest all be lost. With this thought, she turned her full gaze to Jerusalem, lifting up her hands in prayer. As she did, she focused and concentrated in that gaze all the intensity and power of every woman and mother in human history.

On the cross, the terrible darkness descended upon Jesus in all its power. In his extreme weakness, he alternated between blackouts and moments of consciousness. While conscious, he could hear the screams, obscenities and horrible curses of the men being crucified with him. Passersby were taunting him as they returned from work, saying, "If you are the Son of God, come down from the cross" (cf. Matthew 27:42-43). Jesus felt extremely weak and powerless. He wondered what good it was to keep following his Father's will. Doubt tormented him: could God be so cruel and merciless as to abandon him in this way? Where were all his friends? His disciples had all run away, so what future was there to his work? He was tempted to give up the struggle and vent his anger like the criminals who were dying around him. All was black and frustrating despair, and he had little strength left to struggle with it.

After a brief blackout, Jesus' head jerked up and his blood-drenched eyes caught a dim picture of Mary Magdalene in the distance with her hands stretched out to heaven like a tower. Then a vivid childhood image came to Jesus' mind. His mother was out with him in a meadow covered with flowers. A breeze had just sprung up, and she was saying to him, "Son when you breathe, remember the Holy Breath of God, the source of all life. Now take a deep breath." Then Jesus opened his eyes to the full gaze of a dying man. He felt a sudden gust of wind which reminded him of the wind on his baptismal day that brought the fluttering dove upon him, the symbol of love and the Spirit. Jesus took a deep breath which brought him new energy. He stretched out his arms and his body was transfixed with power from a mysterious inner source. He looked around from side to side and cried out in a loud voice, "Abba, Father, I have completed your work" (cf. John 19:30). Then he breathed out his last breath peacefully and calmly.

Far away in Galilee, his mother, too, felt a sudden breeze which came in from the ocean — the wind or breath of the hovering Spirit of God (Genesis 1:1-2). Jesus' mother now felt a calm peace. The cosmic struggle was over. Jesus had triumphed and the New Creation had begun. From the dark clouds over Judea she saw a lightning bolt flash toward the ground. For her, this was the divine energy in the universe being grounded and made available for human beings because Jesus had so completely followed his Father's will. After the lightning, Mary felt a gentle rain. All creation was expressing the inner mystery of the final marriage of Jesus and the Spirit.

Jesus' mother now felt completely at one with her son. The Holy Spirit had always been the guiding love-force of her life, and now the Spirit and Jesus were forever joined together. The complete union of Jesus' will with that of the Father, manifested by Jesus' complete obedience as far as death, had made this possible. The total surrender of Jesus in faith and obedience was matched by a corresponding complete gift of all the Father had — the Holy Spirit.

Back at Golgotha, Mary Magdalene heard the thunder and felt the earth shake as the lightning bolt struck the city of Jerusalem. She, too, felt the gentle rain fall and knew its meaning in a way she could not yet express. She also experienced the mysterious presence of the mother of Jesus at the foot of the cross with her. An extraordinary feeling of oneness joined the two women. By his death, Jesus accomplished the impossible task of joining together his family and his disciples, two groups who had been at odds in the past. John's gospel expressed the meaning of these events by describing Mary Magdalene and Mary the mother of Jesus together at the foot of the cross (19:25-27). Since the other gospels have no hint of Jesus' mother's physical presence but only have Mary Magdalene and her companions, John is probably portraying the inner meaning of events rather than a factual representation.

A great calm and peace descended on the hill of Golgotha. The Roman centurion in charge was deeply impressed with the unusual manner of Jesus' death, and with his confident last cry. He openly proclaimed, "Truly this man was the Son of God" (Mark 15:39).

Mary had no time to reflect on the earthshaking events she had just witnessed. The sun was soon to set, and the Sabbath would begin. The Roman soldiers were concerned that the crucified men be dead and buried before the Jewish Sabbath.

To hasten their death, they came to break the legs of the two other revolutionaries crucified with Jesus. When they came to Jesus, they did not do this because they saw he was already dead. Instead, one of the soldiers routinely pierced his side with a lance, just to make sure he was dead. When he did this, a fount of water and blood gushed out of Jesus' side (John 19:31-34). Mary was struck by this unusual occurrence, but it was not until later that she grasped its deep meaning.

Certain that all three had died, the soldiers quickly took down the bodies to bury them in a common grave in a nearby field. However, a secret disciple of Jesus, Joseph of Arimathea, appeared on the scene with an authorization from Pilate to claim Jesus' body (Mark 15:45-46). Joseph acted with haste, took the body, wrapped it in a linen shroud and placed it in his own family tomb a short distance away. Because the Sabbath began at sunset, they were not able to purchase the spices and ointments needed for a traditional Jewish burial and anointing. Mary Magdalene, however, was determined to do this burial anointment herself as a final demonstration of her affection and love for Jesus. She watched carefully where the body was laid so she could return to the tomb after the Sabbath was over.

11. THE RESURRECTION: THE NEW AGE BEGINS; MARY MAGDALENE AS MYSTICAL SPOUSE

Sabbath Day

"So God blessed the seventh day and hallowed it, because on it he rested from all the work he had done in creation (Genesis 2:3). As God rested and contemplated the work of creation on the Sabbath, so God's people were also to rest and reflect on this day. Mary Magdalene returned to Friday's events, for she considered them God's work of the new Creation. She reflected on each detail and tried to understand its meaning through the Scriptures.

She saw again the great thunder clap and lightning bolt which pierced the sky at Jesus' death. Later she learned that some old sepulchers near Mount Olives were split by this lightning. Stories were told of people receiving visions from the dead. Matthew's gospel takes special note of this:

The earth quaked, boulders split, tombs opened. Many bodies of saints who had fallen asleep were raised. After Jesus' resurrection they came forth from their tombs and appeared to many (27:52-53).

What was the meaning of this? Golgotha (the place of the skull) came to her mind. Golgotha was so named because of the many skulls left there by Roman executions. Another image came of the Scripture passage referring to dry bones. This passage was read during the Passover season. In this prophecy, Ezechiel (37:1-15) had a vision of a plain covered with dry bones. God told the prophet to say to them, "Dry bones, hear the word of the LORD. . . . See I will bring spirit into you, that you may come to life." While the prophet was saying these words, a great commotion like an earthquake or thunder rattled the bones and brought them together. The thunder at Jesus' death on Golgotha, the place of dry bones, echoed this passage in Ezechiel. Originally it referred to Israel, dead in exile, whom God would bring back to new life by a glorious return to their own country. Later, however, the rabbis explained the passage as meaning the last days of history, when God would raise up the dead.

In Jewish tradition, the resurrection of the just was a sure sign of these last days. The prophet Daniel had predicted in his writing: "Many of those who sleep in the dust of the earth shall awake" (12:2). For Mary Magdalene, the events and their Scripture background told her the significance of Jesus' death. The reported visions of the dead were confirmations of the cosmic effects of the death of Jesus on the cross. The New Age had begun.

Another striking occurrence of Friday also deeply impressed her. John's gospel describes it in this way:

> When they came to Jesus and saw that he was already dead, they did not break his legs. One of the soldiers thrust a lance into his side, and immediately blood and water flowed forth (19:33-34).

The last day of the autumn feast of Sukkot or Booths was a
special time when the Jews remembered their deliverance from
death in Sinai by God's provision of miraculous water and bread.
Mary Magdalene recalled Jesus' words during the last time he
came to Jerusalem for this feast:

> If anyone thirst, let him come to me and drink. He
> who believes in me, as the Scripture said, "Out of
> his heart shall flow rivers of living water" (John 7:37-
> 38).

In the next verse, the gospel narrative provides an explanation of Jesus' words, indicating he was speaking about the Spirit
which believers would receive after Jesus' death and resurrection.

Mary also recalled how Jesus spoke of his own body in terms
of the Temple of God: "Destroy this Temple and in three days
I will raise it up" (2:19). The prophet Ezechiel had described
the great Temple of the future with emphasis on a mysterious
spring rising beneath the altar that carried new life to the
world. This inexhaustible spring became a stream and then a
great river that flowed down the Judean slopes into the Dead
Sea. The power and abundance of this river turned the vast
sea of salt into a huge fresh water lake that watered the whole
valley around it. Thus a new Garden of Eden sprang up with
fruit trees so prolific that they produced fruit all during the
year. All this abundance flowed from the mysterious source
underneath the Temple Sanctuary. Ezechiel was speaking of
the Spirit which would flow from the New Temple in the Messianic Age (cf. Ezechiel 47:1-12).

Mary now understood the importance of the fountain of water
and blood issuing from the side of Jesus: it was a sign that
Jesus had become this new Temple and source of the Spirit for
believers. During the Sukkot feast in Jerusalem, Jesus promised that living waters would flow from his heart. Now it became

a reality. Just as Jesus promised a baptism of the Spirit for his followers, now it happened. Along with Jesus' mother, Mary Magdalene also understood that Jesus and the Spirit were now one. Jesus could now pour this, his Spirit, on his followers. For Mary Magdalene, the Spirit in her heart and Jesus of Nazareth were one and inseparable. On the next day, Sunday, she would realize the full implications of this.

Easter Morning

The Sabbath day observance ended at sunset. Mary Magdalene and her companions bought the oils and spices necessary for the burial anointment of Jesus. The hasty burial of Jesus on Friday before sunset, the beginning of the Sabbath, had forced them to omit these burial rites. Next morning, before sunrise, Mary Magdalene and the other women came to the tomb (Mark 16:1-2). Incidentally, John's gospel mentions Mary Magdalene alone at the tomb, emphasizing her special presence as a model or exemplar of the true believer (20:1-18). Arriving at the tomb, Mary was shocked to find the circular stone at the cave's entrance rolled aside. At first she suspected a grave robbery had occurred. Immediately she ran to notify Peter and "the other disciple Jesus loved." Both of them ran to the sepulcher, finding the body missing, but no signs of it being stolen: the shroud was lying on the ground, and the head covering was rolled in a place by itself. No tomb robbers would have taken the time to unwrap the body and leave everything so neatly.

The events described in the gospel are understood only if the reader keeps in mind that the gospel writers believed they were dealing not with a *resuscitation,* but with a *resurrection.* A resuscitation is a return to a normal human existence following an apparent or clinical death. A biblical resurrection is a new form of human existence, no longer under the restrictions of space and time, but under the Spirit. Paul calls this resurrected body a *soma pneumatikon* (spirit-infused body) in contrast to

our natural bodies (1 Corinthians 15:44). This new human existence does not lend itself to inspection and scientific examina-
tion. The risen Jesus appears behind locked doors and disap-
pears (John 20:19-29). Jesus is not recognized even by his best
friends until he makes himself known (John 20:15; 21:4; Luke
24:16). Resurrection appearances are perceived by earthly eyes
only when Jesus chooses to manifest himself. These appearances are meant for those who are ready to see him because of
their faith.

With the sudden shock of not finding the body of Jesus, Mary
stood in front of the tomb overwhelmed. She bent down to look
again inside the tomb and saw two angels in bright robes sitting
at the head and foot of the place where Jesus' body had been.
They said, "Woman, why are you weeping?" (20:13). Mary replied, "Because they have taken away my Lord, and I do not
know where they have laid him." Turning around, she saw a
man standing there whom she took to be the gardener, not
recognizing him as Jesus. He said to her, "Woman, why are
you weeping? Whom do you seek?" She replied to him, "Sir, if
you have taken him away, tell me where you have laid him
and I will take him away." By the repetition of Mary's words,
the gospel writer is impressing on his readers Mary's ardent
longing to see the Jesus she loved so much.

> Jesus said to her, "Mary." She turned and said to
> him in Hebrew "Rabboni!" (which means Teacher).
> Jesus said to her, "Do not hold me, for I have not yet
> ascended to the Father. But go to my brethren and
> say to them, I am ascending to my Father and your
> Father, to my God and your God" (20:16-17).

Only when Jesus calls Mary by name does she recognize him.
His initiative makes her recognition possible. The writer draws
special attention to the encounter by recalling the exact word
that Mary used in Aramaic, *Rabboni,* meaning Master or

Teacher. Mary Magdalene is privileged to be the first to see Jesus because of her great love for him. Now she is given the unique mission to be the first to announce to others that Jesus has risen.

Beneath this event lies a Scriptural meaning which will have a dramatic effect on Mary Magdalene and the gospel audience. During the Passover season, the love poems of the Song of Songs were read in the synagogue. As people listened to the songs that bride and bridegroom recited to one another, they thought of God's own love for his people Israel. John's description of the meeting of Mary and Jesus seems based on one of these poems:

> On my bed by night I sought him whom my soul loves. I sought him but found him not. . . . I will rise then and go about the city; in the streets and squares I will seek him whom my heart loves. I sought him but found him not. The watchmen found me as they went about the city: Have you seen him whom my soul loves? Scarcely had I left them when I found him whom my soul loves. I held him and would not let him go (3:1-4).

The correspondence to the encounter between Mary and Jesus is striking. The following details point to this: the reference to night (John 20:1); the continued searching of the bride for her lover; the question addressed to the watchmen (which is the same word as gardener in Hebrew); finally, the taking hold of him and not willing to let him go. In this manner, John's gospel explains the inner meaning of the relationship between Mary and Jesus. Because the Spirit is in her heart, and Jesus-Spirit are now inseparable, her relationship to Jesus becomes one of mystical spouse. Jesus promised a baptism of the Spirit; she is joined to him as the source of that Spirit.

After years of desiring a deep personal union with Jesus, it becomes a reality for Mary. The gospel singles her out as the model for believers. Jesus had made possible so close an inner union with the Spirit that it could be called a mystical espousal. This was a fulfillment of the Old Testament where the union between God and his people is described in nuptial terms (cf. chap. 4). The apostle Paul used the same terminology in writing to the Corinthians, "I am jealous of you with the jealousy of God himself, since I have given you in marriage to one husband, presenting you as a chaste virgin to Christ" (2 Corinthians 11:2). The book of Revelation pictured the final stage of the kingdom of God as "the wedding day of the Lamb, for his bride has made herself ready" (19:7).

Jesus' ascension (his return to God) was a matter of celebration not just for Mary but for all Jesus' community as well. So she reported to them, "I have seen the Lord," telling them all that had happened (John 20:18). On that Sunday evening, they assembled in a secret place and locked the doors, being afraid the Jewish leaders would arrest them also. All the disciples prayed and yearned to see the Master as Mary had seen him. Responding to their prayer, Jesus appeared and greeted them with the words, "Peace be with you. As the Father has sent me, so I send you" (John 20:21). With these words, the disciples understood they were to continue, duplicate and extend the ministry of Jesus to the whole world. They also trusted that they would have the same power the Father had given Jesus.

Jesus then breathed upon them, saying, "Receive the Holy Spirit." The disciples understood immediately. Jesus' promise to baptize them with the Holy Spirit had now become a reality. Jesus' breath was the breath/Spirit/wind of the New Creation — the fullness of the breath/Spirit/wind that had started the creation of the universe. This same life-giving breath formed the first man and woman (Genesis 2:7). Finally, Jesus' followers were sharing the Spirit-dove of Jesus' own baptismal experience. The inner marriage of the Spirit, the deepest secret of Jesus, was now theirs.

Jesus continued, "If you forgive the sins of any, they are forgiven; if you retain the sins of any, they are retained" (20:23). Jesus' own reception of tax collectors, sinners, the sick and infirm had been an external sign of God's own acceptance and forgiveness. This complete forgiveness, resulting from God's love was considered to be reserved for the world's final age. Jeremiah the prophet had predicted such a day when he spoke in God's name saying that there would be a new covenant in the last days, a new religion of the heart: "They shall all know me from least to greatest, says the LORD, for I will forgive their iniquity, and I will remember their sin no more" (31:34).

Now Jesus' community was empowered to continue his mission. Their acceptance of others into their community would be a sign of the presence of the Holy Spirit, a Spirit of love and forgiveness. Mary Magdalene as a repentant sinner knew that loving forgiveness was the Risen Jesus/Holy Spirit's presence.

The First Pentecost

Meanwhile in Galilee, Jesus' mother and family prepared to leave for Jerusalem, knowing the Holy City was an essential element in the unfolding drama of the New Age. Although Mary was convinced of Jesus' resurrection, there were now other confirmations, including a surprising one within the family circle itself. The Risen Jesus had appeared to James, her oldest son after Jesus (1 Corinthians 15:7). James was a dedicated observer of the Torah, a model of honesty and uprightness, as well as being a man of intense prayer. Later in Jerusalem he would be called James the just and become the spiritual leader of the Jerusalem community for many years.

When Mary and the family arrived in Jerusalem, they brought a new energy and enthusiasm to the disciples. The latter rejoiced that the Spirit of God, the great Spirit of oneness had made possible this unexpected union of Jesus' family and themselves as a result of Jesus' resurrection. Mary not only bore a close physical resemblance to Jesus, but an inner resemblance due to her profound understanding and awareness of the Spirit.

The Acts of the Apostles highlights the first forty days after the Passover/Resurrection of Jesus as an important formative period in the early Christian community. During these days, many apparitions of the Risen Jesus culminated in an Ascension vision forty days after Easter (Acts 1:3-11). The resurrection of Jesus does not fit into the limitations of space and time. Immediately following his death, Jesus "ascended" or entered the divine realm, becoming one with the Spirit. Three days after his death, there were important visions, especially the one to Mary Magdalene. However, there was no "waiting period" between the death and resurrection of Jesus. Luke's story of a 40th day ascension apparition meant to convey to the disciples what happened to Jesus, and what was happening to them: Jesus, now totally with God, was also in them, offering the courage to share the good news with the world.

Jesus' mother led the community in prayer for ten days before the feast of Pentecost. This Jewish feast was celebrated fifty days after the Passover as a special commemoration of God's gift of the Torah not only to Israel but to the world. Mary felt this first Pentecost would inaugurate the little community into a world ministry. In the large upper room of another woman called Mary, there were 120 disciples gathered together. These included the twelve, the Galilean and Judean disciples, Jesus' family and a large number of women. Luke writes, "All these with one accord devoted themselves to prayer with the women and Mary the mother of Jesus and with his brethren" (Acts 1:14).

Mary Magdalene experienced joy in praying with the Mother of Jesus. Their previous communion now blossomed into a visible oneness apparent to others. Each day, as Pentecost approached, their prayers and expectations became more intense.

Finally,

> When the day of Pentecost had come, they were all
> together in one place. And suddenly a sound came
> from heaven like the rush of a mighty wind and it
> filled all the house where they were sitting. And there
> appeared to them tongues as of fire, distributed and
> resting on each of them. And they were filled with
> the Holy Spirit and began to speak in other tongues
> (Acts 2:1-4).

Mary Magdalene felt the Spirit's flame penetrate her being.
This web of fire united her to Jesus' mother, the twelve and
all in the room. She became especially aware of the Spirit in
other persons as well as herself. The Spirit, inseparable from
Jesus, was present in each person. It was not only the Spirit
of Jesus, but the Spirit of his mother, of Peter, of James, and
of all others also. The light-fire of the Spirit illumined each
person. Jesus had hinted of this in describing his Father as
the God of Abraham, the God of Isaac, and the God of Jacob
(Matthew 22:32). His Father was not the God of all summed
up, but the God of each in a unique way. The gust of wind
sweeping the room made Mary Magdalene feel the continuity
of her experience with the wind-spirit which swept over the
oceans of creation, and the wind that brought the fluttering
dove over Jesus at his baptism. It was all one and the same
Spirit.

Mary Magdalene and the others began to experience a new
sense of boldness, daring and confidence. Previously they stayed
indoors, fearing the Jewish leaders. Now they were impelled
by the Spirit to go out and share their good news with everyone.
Their enthusiasm was expressed in joyful song and in a mysterious ecstatic prayer from their hearts which bubbled up as a
new common language of the Spirit. To outsiders it seemed
they were speaking in foreign tongues.

Outside, the crowds that had come for the feast were filling the streets. There were people with white faces of Europe, black of Africa, brown of the Middle East and yellow of the Orient. The streets belonged not only to Jerusalem but to the whole world. Filled with the Spirit, the disciples walked outdoors and mingled with the crowds, announcing the joyful news of the New Age. Many people who had been secret followers of Jesus came out into the open, praising him publicly. In ecstatic praises, they joined their voices to those of the upper room. A new common language of the Spirit united a separated and splintered humanity.

In describing this dramatic scene, the gospel writer Luke recalled the biblical story of the Tower of Babel in Genesis, chapter 11. There humanity in its pride tried to build its own city to reach heaven. By confounding their speech, God made it a *babble* so people could not understand one another. Now God reversed the story of Babel by enabling people to communicate once more through the common medium of the Spirit.

When Mary Magdalene saw the Spirit affect so many men, women and children along with people of many nations, races and social classes, she knew the great Day of the Lord prophesied by Joel had come. God had said,

> Afterward I will pour out my spirit upon all flesh. Your sons and daughters shall prophesy, your old men shall dream, and your young men shall see visions (2:29).

Mary Magdalene now had a better perspective about all that Jesus tried to accomplish. Jesus had spoken a hidden language, the personal language of women and children to bring religion out of the adult male monopoly. Women and children listened to Jesus and understood his message. His female disciples were the only witnesses of all the formative events of his death, burial and resurrection. Women were the founders of the new movement. Now the picture was completed: men and women disciples as well as Jesus' family prayed together that day. Jesus began a great breakthrough of the sexual, national and racial barriers which divided the world into hostile camps. His disciples would continue what he had begun and extend the message of love to the world. By depending on a set of ideas, many ancient philosophers had failed. Instead, the disciples were to trust in the inner dynamism and contagious effects of the shared Spirit of Jesus.

12. MARY MAGDALENE AND THE LOST CHRISTIANS OF THE GNOSTIC GOSPELS

The New Testament offers no further reference to Mary Magdalene after the resurrection story. While an old French tradition tells of her journey to Marseilles and later death there, the legend has Mary carried by the waves and wind in an oarless boat from Israel to the southern coast of France! A more likely possibility is her journey to Ephesus on the west coast of modern Turkey, which claims to have her relics. Ephesus, a large and important trade center, was capital of the Roman province of Asia. Due to the efforts of the Apostle Paul who stayed there for three years, Ephesus had a substantial Christian population. Ephesus was also the probable location of the community of the beloved disciple (the author of John's gospel).

With the growing militarism in Palestine during the time between Jesus' death and war with Rome, 66-70 A.D., Ephesus became a refuge for many Jews and Jewish Christians. John's gospel is the only one that portrays the Mother of Jesus, Mary Magdalene and the beloved disciple at the foot of the cross. This hints at some association between the author and the two women, probably at Ephesus. What we do know for certain is that Mary Magdalene's name and authority were important for gnostic Christians. Some of their documents go back to the second century A.D., indicating that the association with Mary Magdalene may have taken place after her death. Yet since Ephesus was a very important center for the spread of gnostic Christianity, it is possible her association with the movement may have begun during her lifetime.

Within the last ten years, new images of Jesus in addition to those presented by the four gospels have been presented to the general public. The changes began in the mid 1940s with the extraordinary discovery of lost Christian coptic manuscripts in Egypt at Nag Hammadi. At the time of their discovery, their importance was dwarfed temporarily by the discovery of the Dead Sea Scrolls, which revealed the first contemporary documents from the time of Jesus. However, the finds at Nag Hammadi far surpass the Dead Sea Scrolls for the understanding of Jesus and the New Testament. These coptic documents were written around the fourth century A.D., but were translations of much earlier Greek texts. These writings from ancient Christian communities contained a unique view of Jesus never known before.

In 1977, an English edition of these works in a large volume of nearly 500 pages was published. It was called *The Nag Hammadi Library*. Some of the best known books in this collection are the *Gospel of Thomas,* the *Gospel of Philip* and the *Gospel of Truth*. The writings have been called "gnostic" (meaning knowledge) because of their stress on deep personal knowledge and inner enlightenment. In 1981, the paperback edition of the *Gnostic Gospels* by Elaine Pagels was published. Her explanations of Christian gnosticism have reached a wide audience. To understand the beliefs and life-styles of early "gnostic" or "gnostic-oriented" Christians, it is important to sketch the worldview on which they were based.

The following elements are characteristic of the gnostic view, although a universal gnostic teaching never existed. Some Nag

Hammadi books have no Christian orientation, indicating pre-Christian origins. Important for us here are the basic views of Christian "gnostics" on human nature and the universe. "Gnosis" centers on the basic conviction that each person (according to some systems; a select group, according to others) is a microcosm or little universe with the divine, the *pneuma* within them. Most people are "asleep" or unaware of this inner life, and therefore are unable to tap the powerful presence within them. This can only be done through a special kind of inner illumination or "gnosis."

In the gnostic worldview, there is only one Light or God. Through emanation of this light, the world came into existence. This emanation, according to some systems, formed a divine anthropos or primal Man. However, in the process the divine Man or emanated light became divided, scattered and imprisoned within individual human bodies. Most gnostics felt that the human body served as a trap or prison for these divine sparks. For the gnostic Christian, Jesus was a wisdom-type figure who came into this world to help us realize who we really are, and thus be liberated from the bondage of the flesh. "Salvation" consisted in an inner illumination or experience of the divine spark within, together with the "know-how" to escape the domination of hostile evil powers who had revolted from the light and held the world under their domination. Once a person learned to "escape", they could tap the immense powers of their divinity, obtain freedom and immortality, and be united again with the Light from which they came.

The Gnostic Image of Jesus as Teacher

This can be best seen in comparison with the gospels, especially Matthew, Mark and Luke. John's gospel has many similarities to gnostic teachings and may be an attempt to establish a middle point between the other gospels and the gnostic viewpoint. In general, the contrast is between *inner* and *outer*. The gnostics believed each person contained wholeness: all one needed was illumination to discover the divine spark within. In contrast, the "traditional" Christian viewpoint as presented by the gospels presents human beings as needy, sinful and incomplete. To remedy this, Christ comes to bestow what is necessary. The difference can also be expressed in terms of gift or nature. In the gnostic view, individuals are by *nature* sons of God, and Christ comes to assist in this discovery. In the "normal" Christian view, Christ's work is a *gift* or favor bestowed on the individuals themselves.

The authors of the four gospels emphasized the true identity of Jesus and attempted to answer the question, "Who is he?" The central question in Mark's gospel is "Who do you say that I am?"

In contrast, the gnostic gospel of Thomas presents Jesus not as a teacher who comes primarily to tell his disciples *who he is,* but *who they are* because they are identified with him and draw from the same source he draws from:

> Jesus said to his disciples: "Make me a comparison; tell me what I am like." Simon Peter said to him, "You are a righteous angel." Matthew said to him: "You are like a man who is a wise philosopher." Thomas said to him: "My mouth is not capable of stating what you are like." Jesus said: "I am not your master, because you have drunk and become drunk from the same bubbling spring which I have measured out" (*NHL* II, 2:35;2-8).

In the Gnostic Texts, Jesus is indeed divine but teaches our divinity as well. This sense of identification is expressed strongly in the gospel of Philip where a follower of Valentinian (a gnostic teacher) writes,

> You saw the spirit, you became spirit. You saw Christ, you became Christ. You saw (the Father, you)

shall become the Father . . . you see yourself and
what you see you shall (become) (*NHL* II, 3:61, 29-
35).

According to the same author, one who achieves *gnosis* becomes "no longer a Christian, but a Christ."

Jesus as teacher leads the people to the inward search within
themselves to uncover *who they really are*. In the gospel of
Thomas, Jesus says,

If those who lead you say to you, "the kingdom is in
heaven," then the birds of heaven will precede you.
If they say to you, "it is in the sea," then the fish will
precede you. But the kingdom is within you and outside you. When you know yourselves, then you will
be known, and you will know that you are sons of
the living Father (*NHL* II, 2:32, 20-25).

In the first three gospels, Jesus works within everyday life
to transform the world through changing human relationships.
He takes the initiative to call the tax collector, a much hated
Roman puppet, to be a member of his inner circle of apostles
(Matthew 8:1-13). The violence and oppression of their harsh
Roman overlords is to be overcome not by violent resistance,
but by responding to their unjust demands by loving service;
e.g., "Should anyone force you into service for one mile, go with
him two miles" (Matthew 5:24).

However, in the gnostic documents the important matter is
not what you do, but *who you really are.* If you know who you
are and are able to break away from the world, then your
actions will be good. Once people know their inner divine nature
and are enlightened, then national distinctions, Jew, Gentile,
Greek, disappear. Since sex distinctions come from the body
and the visible world, an experience of the inner divine nature
brings about perfect equality, so there is no longer male or

female. So Jesus says in the gospel of Thomas,

> When you make the male and the female one and
> the same, so that the male not be male nor the female
> female . . . then will you enter the kingdom (*NHL*
> II, 2:37, 25-31).

In the canonical gospels, Jesus is concerned with human institutions. He blesses marriage, and advises against divorce. His disciples are a visible and definable group of twelve, whose leader is Peter.

In contrast, the gnostic documents exhibit a strong antipathy for all human institutions as being part of an evil and corrupt world. Some gnostics even forbade marriage for this reason. The Jewish Law, as found in the Bible was condemned because it commanded husband and wife to beget children. This condemnation of marriage is similar to the beliefs of those Christians criticized by the author of the letters to Timothy and Titus. He writes that they "forbid marriage and require abstinence from foods which God created." . . . (1 Timothy 4:3)

Since gnostics trusted in their inner light, they distrusted external authority and teachers. The tractate on *Authoritative Teaching* in the Nag Hammadi Library considers external shepherds as enemies. The true shepherd is the voice of the inner shepherd heard through *gnosis*:

> They (the enemies) did not realize that she (the soul)
> has an invisible, spiritual body; they think "We are
> her shepherd who feeds her." But they did not realize
> that she knows another way which is hidden from
> them. This her true shepherd taught her in *gnosis*
> (*NHL* VI 3:32, 30-33:3).

The gnostic author of the *Apocalypse of Peter* pokes fun at church officials who claim they have special authority from God:

And there shall be others of those who are outside our number who name themselves bishop and also deacons, as if they have received their authority from God. They bend themselves under the judgment of their leaders. Those people are dry canals (*NHL VII*, 3:79, 21-30).

The Christian gnostic movement was not a small splinter group of fringe Christians whose ideas and life-style left no impact on the Christian church as a whole. They were a numerous and influential group. The author of the letters to Timothy and Titus addresses a serious and widespread movement which has strong similarities to that in the Nag Hammadi documents. The "false" teachings are so widespread in Ephesus and Crete that the author complains "all in (the Roman province of) Asia have left me" (2 Timothy 1:15). Irenaeus, a father of the church, devoted most of his life to counter this movement, and wrote his volumes *Adversus Haereses* in the second century to attack their teachings.

Mary Magdalene and the Gnostic Christians

The various gnostic documents do not present a unified teaching, so it would be best to examine separately each one where she receives significant mention. First, the Gospel of Thomas, dated to around 150-200 A.D. There Mary speaks to Jesus once, asking, "Whom are your disciples like" (*NHL* II, 2:36, 34-35). Jesus gives her an enigmatic answer. It is quite significant that the gospel ends with this saying of Jesus addressed to Mary Magdalene. Simon Peter said to Jesus, "Let Mary leave us, for women are not worthy of life." Jesus replied, "I myself shall lead her in order to make her male, so that she, too, may become a living spirit resembling you males. For every woman who will make herself male will enter the kingdom of Heaven (*NHL* II, 2:51, 21-25).

It is interesting here that Mary Magdalene appears as an

adversary to Peter, who wants the Master to send her away. Peter's opposition to Mary is also found elsewhere in the gnostic documents. Jesus answers him by explaining what he will accomplish within Mary. This is a hint that Simon Peter is concerned with outward things and Mary with inward matters. Surfacewise, the words of Jesus to her sound like a sex-change operation, but this is not the case. Jesus is making her "male" to restore her to the original "Man" who is really both male and female, made to the image of God: "God created man in his image; in the divine image he created him; male and female he created them" (Genesis 1:26). The reference to making her a "living spirit" (Genesis 2:7) confirms the relationship to the Genesis texts. It is through union with Jesus that she will recover her true image of God, which combines male and female. This presupposes that Jesus is this "Man" as the perfect combination of the two sexes. Later in the Gospel of Philip this will become more explicit and much more developed.

The meaning of "male" as referring to the first man is taken up elsewhere in Thomas, where Jesus refers to the same process in regard to both men and women. The disciples ask if they will enter the kingdom if they become as little children. Jesus replies,

> When you make the two one, and when you make the inside like the outside and the outside like the inside, the above like the below, and when you make the male and female one and the same, so that the male not be male nor the female female . . . then you will enter the kingdom of heaven (*NHL* II, 2:37, 25-31).

From the brief mention of Mary in the gospel of Thomas, she emerges as a privileged disciple expressing, in contrast to Peter, the inner nature of the kingdom. The androgynous Risen Jesus brings her to completion. He remakes her into what she was at Creation, male and female, a perfect reflection of God. Mary is the exemplar of what each Christian is to become through union with Jesus. Her role, and the role of other women uncovers the feminine side of God.

The gospel of Philip (dated to the third century A.D.) has attracted attention because of the unusual intimate references to Jesus and Mary Magdalene:

> There were three who always walked with the Lord: Mary, his mother, and her sister and the Magdalene, the one who was called a companion. His sister and his mother and his companion were each a Mary (*NHL* II, 3:59, 8-10).

The author goes further to state (words bracketed are those supplied by translators where the manuscript had gaps):

> (But Christ loved) her more than (all) the disciples (and used to) kiss her (often) on her (mouth). The rest of (the disciples were offended) by it (and expressed disapproval). They said to him, "Why do you love her more than all of us?" (*NHL* II, 3:63, 34-64, 5).

While kisses were a usual family greeting, the author hints at more. However, this meaning needs to be understood within the total context of the Gospel of Philip. For Philip, the original cause of evil was the separation of Adam and Eve who originally were one being within the androgynous primeval Man. The author writes, "When Eve was still in Adam, death did not exist. When she was separated from him death came into being" (*NHL* II, 3:68, 23-24). The remedy for this separation is reunion of the two: "If he (Adam) becomes again complete and attains his former self, death will be no more" (*NHL* II, 3:68, 24-26). As a result, we are incomplete beings, only a shadow of our real selves: "(Our flesh) is not true, but (we possess) only an image of the true" (*NHL* II, 3:68, 36-37).

It is the mission of Christ to effect this reunion of male and female within persons so God's image in Genesis can be realized. Christ alone can do this because he is the perfect Man. Philip describes how Christ became this Man:

> The Father of everything united with the virgin who came down, and a fire shone for him on that day. He appeared in the great bridal chamber. Therefore his body came into being that very day. It left the bridal chamber as one who came into being from the bride-groom and the bride (*NHL* II, 3:71, 4ff).

Christ is the complete being and helps Christians to be also. He does this through an inner marriage of which the sacraments, especially baptism, are the symbol: "The Lord (did) everything in a mystery, a baptism, and a chrism, a redemption and a bridal chamber" (*NHL* II, 3:67, 29-30). The agent of this intimate union is "the seed of the Spirit" (*NHL* II, 3:85, 23). Similar to the gospel of John (6:63) the writer says, "his blood is the Holy Spirit (*NHL* II, 3:57, 6-7). Through this intimate union, the believer is not just united *to* Christ, but becomes one with him: "You saw the Spirit, you became Spirit. You saw Christ, you became Christ. You saw (the Father, you) shall become Father (*NHL* II, 3:61, 29-31).

By this nuptial union, the true self is recovered, the original Person in whom both male and female are one: "Through the Holy Spirit we are indeed begotten again, but we are begotten through Christ in the two. We are anointed through the Spirit. When we were begotten, we were united" (*NHL* II, 3:69, 5-9). Because of the inner resemblance to the sexual union between man and woman, Christ's union is called a *kiss:* "For it is by a kiss that the perfect conceive and give birth" (*NHL* II, 3:59, 2-3). For this reason, the author points out the symbolism behind the kisses that Christians exchange: these symbolize the inner kiss they have received at baptism through their nuptial union with Christ: "For this reason we also kiss one another. We receive conception from the grace which is in each other" (*NHL* II, 3:59, 4-5).

This is why the Gospel of Philip gives such attention to Mary Magdalene, her companionship with Jesus and the frequent kisses she received! She is the model or exemplar for the Christian who has understood the depth of meaning of his/her faith. Every believer is another Mary Magdalene who draws on the same inner sources. He/she receives the sacraments as a most intimate nuptial union with Christ enabling them to recover their true nature, of the original Person who combines both male and female, thus becoming the complete image of God.

Once again, as in Thomas, we can note the importance of Mary in bringing out this inner feature of the Risen Jesus' mission. She is the model for the believer as she becomes companion and mystical spouse of Jesus. Just as man and woman unite sexually, each person has a heavenly counterpart, the Risen Jesus, to whom they are united in the sacramental nuptial chamber.

In addition, Philip emphasizes the recovery of the feminine element within human beings. He writes,

> Adam came into being from two virgins, from the Spirit and from the virgin earth. Christ, therefore, was born from a virgin to rectify the fall which occurred in the beginning (*NHL* II, 3:71, 16-21).

Note the connection of the feminine with the virginal, motherly earth.

The Gospel of Mary is a third document in which Mary Magdalene is prominent. In fact, the whole gospel is about her, and the special message Christ entrusted her for the world. This document was not only a coptic manuscript, but a Greek fragment dated to the beginning of the third century. The first six pages of the coptic are missing. From the remaining pages we can gather that they were the beginning of a farewell discourse of Jesus, who is about to leave this earth. As a final greeting he says,

> Peace be with you. Receive my peace to yourselves. Beware that no one lead you astray, saying, "Lo, here or Lo, there!" For the Son of Man is within you. Follow after him! Those who seek him will find him. Go then and preach the gospel of the kingdom. Do not lay down any rules beyond what I appointed for you, and do not give a law like the law-giver lest you be constrained by it" (*NHL,* BG 7, 14 — 9,4).

Note again the typical gnostic emphasis on the inward: "The Son of Man is within you, Follow after him! Those who seek him will find him." Also their typical fear of laws, rules and regulations is evident.

In the story, after Jesus left the disciples, they were afraid. They began to weep, and wondered how they could begin to preach, especially since they might have to suffer as the Master did. At this point Mary Magdalene intervened and "turned their hearts to the Good, and they began to discuss the words of the (Savior)" (9.20-23). Peter turned to Mary and said, "Sister, we know that the Savior loved you more than the rest of women. Tell us the words of the Savior which you remember — which you know (but) we do not nor have we heard them" (10, 1-5). Mary answered them and said,

> What is hidden from you I will proclaim to you. And she began to speak to them these words: "I", she said, "saw the Lord in a vision and I said to him, 'Lord, I saw you today in a vision' " (10.6-10).

Unfortunately, at this point there are four pages missing in the manuscript. From the little remaining of her account, it is not possible to reconstruct its principal content. At the end of her address to the disciples, Mary becomes silent. Some of the disciples question the validity of her words. Andrew says to the others,

> Say what you (wish to) say about what she has said.
> At least I do not believe that the Savior said this.
> For certainly these teachings are strange ideas (17, 10-16).

Peter then jumps in to support his brother Andrew, and asks this question, "Did he really speak privately with a woman and not openly to us? Are we to turn about and all listen to her? Did he prefer her to us?" (17, 17-23).

Mary broke down into tears and said to Peter, "My brother Peter, what do you think? Do you think that I thought this up myself in my heart or that I am lying about the Savior?" (18, 1-5). Then Levi, the humble tax collector rallied to her defense and said,

> Peter, you have always been hot-tempered. Now I see you contending against the woman like the adversaries. But if the Savior found her worthy, who are you indeed to reject her? Surely, the Savior knows her very well. That is why he loved her more than us. Rather let us be ashamed and put on the perfect man, and separate as he commanded us and preach the gospel, not laying down any other rule, or other law beyond what the Savior said (18, 6-21).

The Gospel of Mary ends with the disciples going out to proclaim and preach the good news.

Despite the missing fragments, the gospel of Mary indicates Jesus revealed a special message to Mary, and the apostles ought to preach this message to the world. Her closeness to Jesus, and the secrets he told her, give Mary the prerogative to instruct even the twelve. Once again she is set in opposition to Peter, Andrew and others, although Levi defends her. The message Mary has received is inner-directed. The Savior announces to all that the Son of Man is within, and the disciples should not be deceived by those who say he is outside (probably in the form of external shepherds). In the opening address, the Savior emphasizes they are not to create new laws or rules, and this is repeated at the end by Levi.

Because of the missing pages, we have only a hint of Mary's message in the words of Levi that they are to "put on the perfect man" — which may be a reminder of the gnostic interpretation of the Genesis story as presented in Philip's gospel. Once again, in the gospel of Mary, it is a woman who is the unique and preferred bearer of revelation in preference to all the male disciples, including Peter.

13. THE OTHER WOMEN IN JESUS' LIFE

Martha and Mary

In Luke's gospel, these two sisters have a home in an unidentified village. Jesus and his disciples visit them and receive hospitality (10:38-42). For those times, it was very unusual for Jesus to enter a home where there are only two women. Luke tells the story in view of a concern for women shown throughout his gospel, often called "the gospel of women." Luke himself is probably a Gentile convert to Christianity (Colossians 4:11-14). In Luke's Greek environment, women had considerably more freedom than in the Jewish world. Through his experience as a missionary, Luke had seen that women have played a very important part in the spread of the gospel.

However, when Luke reviewed his sources (1:1-3), he found a predominance of men's stories. He was anxious to correct this in any way he could. Consequently, he highlights women in his gospel. It is Elizabeth, the Baptist's mother, who first believes the news of his coming birth, despite the physical impossibility of conception due to her old age (1:24-25; 57-60). Mary, the mother of Jesus, is the model for all believers at any time: "Blessed is she who has believed" (1:45). This is because she accepted the impossible — even a virginal conception (1:38). In her joyful song of praise, the *Magnificat,* Mary is a representative figure summing up the hopes and aspirations of her people as a humble servant of God (1:47-55). Anna, a prophetess, is inspired to meet Mary and Joseph when they come to Jerusalem to present the child to the Lord (1:36-38).

In the public ministry of Jesus, Luke presents stories about women found nowhere else in the gospels: the resurrection of the only son of a widow (7:11-17); the story of the penitent woman who washes Jesus' feet with her tears (7:36-50). Only Luke notes that Mary Magdalene, Joanna and Susanna, along with other women, accompany Jesus on his journeys and provide for him out of their own means (8:1-3). Likewise Jesus' visit to Martha and Mary is only in Luke 10:38-42; also, the cure of the woman on the Sabbath (13:10-17); the parable of the woman with the lost coins (15:8-10); the story of the widow and persevering prayer; finally, Jesus' words to the daughters of Jerusalem on the way to the cross (23:28-29).

In Luke, the story of Martha and Mary is included to answer a very important question in the early church: what is to be the position and role of a woman in the Christian community? Luke presents a strong contrast between Martha and Mary. Mary is seated at the Lord's feet, listening to his word. To be "seated at the Lord's feet" is a technical expression for a disciple (cf. 8:35). On the other hand, "Martha was distracted about much serving." Martha is fulfilling the traditional woman's role of serving the men, children and family.

Martha is not in any way criticized for this. However, she is upset that Mary is not helping her — that Mary is not doing what a woman *should* be doing. She asks Jesus to *command* Mary to come out and help: She went out to him (Jesus) and said, "Do you not care that my sister has left me to serve alone. Tell her then to help me." Jesus refuses to comply. Luke is telling us through this story that there is no *command* of Jesus in the early church that women must keep to their traditional role to be good Christians. But the question still remains whether this is not preferable, though not a command. So Jesus answers, "Martha, Martha, you are anxious and troubled about many things; one thing is needful. Mary has chosen the good portion, which shall not be taken from her."

There is some textual difficulty in the Greek manuscripts about the phrase "one thing is needful." Some texts read "a few things." This is probably due to the seemingly absolute answer "one thing," which creates difficulties. However, "the one thing necessary" is not an exclusive expression, but a preferential one. Martha is not being put down in any way. Her role of loving family service and hospitality is a following of Jesus. However, Mary's choice to listen to Jesus' word, independent of the traditional woman's role of service is even more important. For Luke's day and age this is a radical teaching.

Martha and Mary are also known by the author of the fourth gospel but the story as in Luke is not found there. In John's gospel, Martha and Mary illustrate the personal relationship of Jesus to his disciples, especially women. This is found in the story of Lazarus' resurrection, only related by John 11:1-44. In the story, Jesus is outside of Judea when news arrives about the serious illness of Lazarus, the brother of the two women. Jesus' relationship to the two sisters is described in this way: "Now Jesus loved Martha and her sister and Lazarus" (11:5). This love is so great that he is willing to risk his life by going to Judea to help them. He is willing to lay down his life for his sheep, as he says in 10:11. After two days (during which time Lazarus dies) Jesus says to his disciples, "Let us go into Judea again." The disciples know very well what this could mean and respond, "Rabbi, the Jews are now seeking to stone you and are you going there again?" (11:7) Finally, Thomas says, "Let us go that we may die with him" (11:16).

When Jesus arrives at Bethany, a group of friends are mourning at the home of the two sisters. Martha goes out to meet Jesus and says,

Lord, if you had been here, my brother would not
have died. And even now I know that whatever you
ask from God, God will give you. Jesus said to her,
"Your brother will rise again." Martha said to him,
"I know he will rise again in the resurrection at the
last day" (11:21-24).

The gospel story is preparing the way for the great act of
faith Martha will make. She is faced with the crisis of death,
the ultimate last enemy. Yet she still trusts that God will give
her *anything* she asks. Jesus assures her that her brother will
rise again, but Martha understands this in reference to the
traditional Jewish belief in the resurrection that will occur in
the last days of history.

Jesus then said to her,

I am the resurrection and the life s/he who believes
in me, though s/he die yet s/he shall live and whoever
lives and believes in me shall never die (11:25).

In effect, Jesus tells her that the last days she awaits are
not far off in the future but right now. This is the message
Jesus preached when he announced that the Kingdom of God
was at hand. If so, the resurrection and eternal life are available
here and now. Then Jesus addresses the challenging question
to Martha and (also to the audience of John's gospel). "Do you
believe this?" Martha responds, "Yes, Lord; I believe you are
the Christ, the Son of God, he who is coming into the world"
(11:27).

It is striking that the great confession of faith (spoken by
Peter, a man, in Matthew 16:16) is made here by Martha, a
woman. John is telling us that Jesus goes to the ultimate —
as far as death — to prove his love for a disciple, as represented
by Martha. Martha in return responds by a total act of faith
and surrender to Jesus' word by believing even the impossible,

the resurrection of her brother Lazarus (who likewise represents the dead believer).

Martha at this point goes to call her sister Mary, saying, "The Teacher is here and is calling for you" (11:28). Mary rose quickly and went out to meet Jesus. Here Mary represents the *listening* disciple who hears Jesus' call and obeys. Jesus had said that the Good Shepherd calls his sheep by name (10:3). Her meeting with Jesus is more intense than that of Martha. She fell at his feet and said, like Martha, "Lord, if you had been here, my brother would not have died" (11:32). She is unable to speak further because she becomes choked up with tears. On seeing this, Jesus himself begins to cry, so much so that some people who were mourning with Mary said, "See how much he loved him." Others, however, said, "Could not he who opened the eyes of the blind man have kept this man from dying?" (11:36-37) With this, Jesus goes to Lazarus' tomb, moved by deep emotion. He prays to his heavenly Father and then with a loud voice commands, "Lazarus, come forth."

Like Martha, Mary is the type of disciple who believes and trusts even in the face of what appears to be completely impossible. She is too choked with emotion to speak like her sister Martha. However, she does not need to. Jesus completely understands and responds to the deepest desires in her heart (and those in every human being, in the mind of the evangelist).

Only in John's gospel both Mary and Martha appear in the account of the Bethany supper (12:1-7). Luke omits the Bethany anointing, and Matthew and Mark have an unnamed woman, whom we named in Chapter 7 as being most probably Mary Magdalene. There are reasons to believe that John's account, as a later rendering of the Bethany story, is not as accurate as the earlier accounts in Matthew and Mark. Scholars believe that the fourth gospel has put together here several originally separate stories: one is the account of the woman anointing Jesus' feet at the house of Simon (cf. Luke 7:36-50). It is only John that has an anointing of Jesus' *feet* at Bethany. A second source is the Martha and Mary story as found in Luke 10:38-42. Both Luke and John describe Martha as one who *serves* at table. A third is the Bethany dinner story as found in Matthew and Mark, where it is a head anointing. Regardless, however, of the original form of the story, John's gospel wishes to make the point that Mary of Bethany represents the perfect disciple because she understands that Jesus is willing to die for his people, and responds to this with a deep expression of love through the anointing of Jesus.

Simon Peter's Mother-in-Law

The gospels focus special attention on the cure of Simon's mother-in-law because Simon's house became the new home of Jesus after he was forced to leave Nazareth (Luke 4:30-31). Mark tells the story very simply:

> And immediately he left the synagogue and entered the house of Simon and Andrew with James and John. Now Simon's mother-in-law lay sick with a fever; and immediately they told him of her. And he came and took her by the hand and lifted her up and the fever left her; and she served them (1:29-31).

Jesus returned again and again to this new home where he could always feel at home, despite the rejection at Nazareth. Peter's mother-in-law, as an older woman, would be the one in charge of the women's activities of ministering to and serving the family. The story ends by simply noting that "she served them" in her traditional woman's role. In this new family of disciples, she would be one of the special people that Jesus would call "mother" (Mark 3:34-35).

Salome, the Mother of the Sons of Zebedee

Another woman Jesus called by the affectionate title of

"mother" was Salome, the mother of James and John, two of Jesus' closest disciples. Peter, James and John were a special inner group of disciples who were associated with Jesus at a number of very important moments of his life; e.g., at his transfiguration, at his prayer in the garden, and during his prediction of the destruction of the temple. The three of them, along with Andrew, were the first disciples called by Jesus according to Mark 1:16-20 (for another version see John 1:35-42). The home of James and John was another home very familiar to Jesus and their mother was the heart of that household. According to Matthew, this woman was faithful to Jesus right to the end. She was with him in his final journey to Jerusalem (20:20) and was one of the few women mentioned by name as witnesses of his crucifixion (27:56). She was also one of the three faithful women, including Mary Magdalene, who came to anoint his body on Easter Sunday morning (Mark 16:1).

The "Other Mary"

This Mary is the mother of James and Joseph, who were probably early disciples of Jesus. She is the only woman, except for Mary Magdalene, named three times in Matthew and Mark: at his death, burial and on Easter Sunday. Matthew refers to her as the "other Mary" (27:61; 28:1). She must have been a close disciple of Jesus as well as a special friend and companion of Mary Magdalene. She may be the same Mary (the wife) of Clopas mentioned in John 19:25.

Other Women

Joanna, a prominent woman, wife of the steward of King Herod, is named only by Luke as a woman who accompanied Jesus on his journeys and helped to support Jesus and his disciples out of her own financial means (8:2-3). Luke also names her as one of the women who comes with Mary Magdalene to the tomb of Jesus on Easter morning (24:10).

Luke also names Susanna along with Joanna in the above text as one of the women who accompanied Jesus and provided for the disciples from her own means.

Mary, the mother of Jesus, also has a sister who is named only in the gospel of John as being with Mary at the foot of the cross (19:25).

The dialogue with the woman of Samaria is only found in John's gospel 4:1-42. This woman had come to a well to perform her traditional task of carrying water to the home. She had been married five times and was at the moment living with a man who was not her husband. She must have had a notorious reputation in her home town. Somehow Jesus knew about all this (4:18) and took the initiative to talk to her and invite her to be a disciple To do this Jesus had to break through some very strong racial and sexual barriers. First of all she was a woman and it was not customary to talk to strange women in public. When his disciples returned from the village after purchasing food, "they marveled that he was talking with a woman" (4:27). Secondly, she was a stranger and a foreigner. The Samaritans were only part Jewish by race, and were regarded as Gentiles. Often they were not even on speaking terms. The Jews excluded them from the temple because they had broken the laws on inter-marriage with non-Jews. The Samaritans in turn built their own temple and place of worship on a mountain near Samaria.

It is especially unusual that this woman went around the town to tell people about Jesus and was instrumental in bringing many Samaritans to belief in Jesus. John writes, "Many Samaritans from the city believed in him because of the woman's testimony" (4:39). One of the greatest events in early Christianity was the first breakthrough to a non-Jewish group that came about through the conversion of many Samaritans (Acts 8:4-25). The fourth gospel traces their first contact with Jesus to the work of this extraordinary woman, about whom nothing else is known.

14. SEX/SPIRIT IN THE NEW AGE: A MODERN EPILOGUE

How much has really changed over the last two thousand years? At first glance, the situation of women today hardly resembles that in the time of Jesus. In most countries of the Western world, women are no longer tied either to their husbands or fathers. Women have achieved considerable freedom, though not equality, in the economic, social and religious sections of today. Yet regardless of external advances in business and education, the inner images of woman have changed little in many societies for thousands of years. We find countless examples in radio, television, cinema and literature of an image (held by both sexes) where woman should look up to, and *please* a man. Significantly, while the modern woman's liberation movement has been a step forward, it has also generated problems. This movement has made it possible for some women to find meaningful careers in the public world. However, it also means that many women have little time for the personal world of home and family, and *men have not filled in this gap.*

In other words, what is needed is a human liberation movement where men can step in and share equal responsibility with women in the caring and raising of children. When this is done, both can share, each on a part-time basis, the public

138

world of work. The ones who have suffered most from the absence of both men and women have been the children. Shared responsibility for them means creating a society whose roots grow out of personal care by father and mother. If the New Age means "there is no longer male or female" (Galatians 3:28), then this new age simply has not yet come.

With this in mind, we can look back to the essential message of Jesus as understood by women and outline some special areas of emphasis. Jesus' message and life-style were not concerned with what we call a "woman's liberation" movement today. It could be better termed an effort toward human liberation. In speaking of "man" or "woman" we do not necessarily mean male and female but the masculine and feminine within each person. In Jesus' time, the "feminine" world was one of personal service in the home. Jesus' intention was to draw the average man back into this feminine world that was so much a part of himself. In this way, he could achieve an inner personal integration and break through the walls that confined him to the "man's world" of that day.

Hope cannot blossom until we deal seriously with a basic root disease which is sapping the strength of the human race. The disease exists in the images men and women have of one another, especially the image of woman. The image of woman has been built up in our minds for countless centuries. It is an image filled with emotion and power which prevents us from seeing men and women as they really are. It is based on a complex interconnected set of models and expectations of what she *should* do and how she *should* behave, act and even look. Unless we change these images at their roots we can never expect to have peace and justice in our world.

How did early Christians deal with this problem? We have seen that gnostic Christians did not believe that the Risen Jesus was a *male* savior. They believed that after his resurrection, the Spirit made him into the perfect human being as Man/Woman. These Christians felt the work of God was to bring each person to the full divine image which is male and female according to Genesis 1:26. There is also evidence in earlier documents that points to the same view. Only 25 years after Jesus' death, Paul wrote the Galatians that those who are baptized "put on" Christ, and as a result there "is neither male nor female, for you are all one in Christ Jesus" (3:28). Paul pointed to something deep and internal that comes through union with Christ — the source of the Spirit.

The letter to the Ephesians, written before the end of the first century, directs the believer to "put on that new man created in God's image, whose justice and holiness are born of the truth" (4:23). Note how the term "new man" is connected with God's image (male and female) in Genesis. Jesus himself appealed to the same text in Genesis when he stressed the equality of man and woman in regard to marriage laws. He said, "Have you not read that the Creator from the beginning made them male and female . . ." (Matthew 19:4).

The following specific applications to this basic equality are offered as suggestions toward the integration of masculine and feminine within each person.

1. The feminine side tends to be more inward, connected to the inner sources of life: fertility, nurturing, earth, sun and moon. It is personally oriented. The masculine side tends to be more outer-directed, concerned with thoughts, mind organization, things, rather than people. Since this is the world of power and control, it tends to suppress the other side. If the feminine side loses its influence in society, the result is a society that goes to the extreme in emphasizing science, technology and progress to the detriment of human sensitivity. Such a society caused the terrible holocaust of over six million Jews in Nazi Germany in the second world war. Such a society continues to manufacture nuclear weapons, supplying the world with more and more munitions until it becomes one huge armed camp.

A radical antidote for this weapon madness is to be involved in the world of children. They are the best teachers. Children embody a sense of wonder and enjoy each day's happenings, be they as simple as sunrise and sunset. Children do not live in an exclusive world of things and projects, but in a world of wholeness that is both male and female. This is why both the gospels and the gnostic documents place great emphasis on becoming like little children.

2. The restoration of friendship between man and woman, husband and wife. True friendship blossoms only among equals. Frequently, "love" between men and women is not based on this inner equality but on a role, model or expectation that one partner has for the other. It may be based on physical attraction, sexual pleasure, parental modeling or whatever. These expectations are external, built on ideas and models in the mind. They are not in the person himself/herself. When masculine and feminine are not integrated at the inner level it creates a void. To attempt to fill this vacuum, we often try to make the outside man or woman into a god or goddess. No person can live up to god or goddess models. Note that the words "I adore you" are found in many love songs. We try to make the other person fulfill what is lacking inside and this is a great strain for human beings to bear. Those who achieve real inner integration find themselves able to relate on a friendship basis not only with the opposite sex but with their own sex as well. By *giving* to one another of their fullness, they overcome the inordinate thirst of having to continually *receive* to fulfill their inner needs.

3. In the biblical Song of Songs a close connection exists between the feminine and the animals, the land, mother-earth and all creation. The woman's womb is a funnel descending into the mysterious powers of earth and life. Jesus also entered into this side of himself through a free and aware expression of his own human emotions. He could cry when he saw Jerusalem and pictured the evils of war that would come upon the city (Luke 19:41). He could be angry when he saw people

ready to accuse him for healing on the Sabbath (Mark 3:5). In addition, it is the feminine side of humans that is most open to art, music, dancing and the deepest expressions of the human psyche.

Ars gratia artis (art for its own sake) is an old Latin adage. Art is not ulterior-motivated, nor does art belong to the domain of mind, comparison and judgment. Art reaches deep levels within which are connected to the universe's heart. Penetrating the mysterious web of interconnection, art binds together the universe. By developing the feminine side through art, human beings become more sensitive to one another and to all of life. Without art, people become ulterior motivated in everything whether for money, esteem or security. Art is being who we are and allowing ourselves to experience this and the world without regard to time. Art is really the timeless dimension of life. The worth of any human civilization can be judged by the value it places on art in all its various expressions as music, poetry and dance.

Overdevelopment of the masculine side takes away from the earth and concentrates us excessively in the mind's realm where ideas flourish. Overstress of the mind leads to focusing on comparisons, judgments, competition and finally moves toward war. Most of the gods of war have been masculine. In contrast, the essence of Jesus' message was a peace movement which was understood by the feminine world. Women are the greatest casualties of war, for they feel most the losses of children and spouses. Jesus' religion is a religion of the heart, not of the mind with a vast collection of precepts, laws and directions. As a way of living, it is nonviolence and loving in a practical, concrete way. Jesus stressed that the woman's world of personal and loving service was to be the model for everyone. Through actions like the washing of feet, Jesus acted on this belief.

4. In the realm of religion: A great struggle of Jesus was with the male religious establishment of his day. Their control, exercised for countless centuries reinforced the prevailing image of

YHWH as essentially a male god, with his warrior's role. He was YHWH, God of hosts, head of heavenly and earthly armies. The Scriptures were written by men and mostly for men who led prayer, worship and fulfilled all the positive religious laws. (Women were obliged only to the negative precepts.) Once again, have times significantly changed? Where we find an exclusive or predominant male leadership in religion, we usually see emphasis on the masculine or outer side of religion, stressing externals and observances, rather than on the intuitive inner Spirit. Such leadership cannot help but cause people to believe that the male leader represents a *male* Savior. The alternative is seeing Christ as the Spirit-infused androgynous human being and model for the male-female image of God. Through the centuries, the image of God has helped many Christians to counteract the overwhelming male models in the external church.

5. When we appreciate the Spirit/Risen Jesus as working to create the full human person, we discover new possibilities for ecumenism among the world religions. It is the outer "masculine oriented" elements that have led to separation, exclusivism and even wars to defend or promulgate doctrines, religious formulations, and teachings. The mystics (those who have reached the inner heart of religion) have always felt close to one another. This is because they have drunk together from the same mysterious inner Source.

This does not mean that doctrines are not important. The point is that religious formulations may distinguish but they should never separate what is the root. Every religious tradition is a distinct and beautiful branch united to the same trunk and nourished through common roots by the water of the Spirit. Uniformity kills because it immediately separates and excludes others. True oneness is only possible when diversity is recognized and appreciated. External conformity is not a living unity but an enforced control.

6. A deepening of the feminine side of religion and of individuals balances the encroaching masculine, and leads to a person-

centered religion. God is seen in and through human beings as they grow more and more to become mature persons. In this process, every person's face becomes a mirror of God. The Spirit of unique human beings open to knowing and loving. Jesus knew the "God of Abraham, Isaac and Jacob." I come to know God as the Spirit of my spouse, my friend, my fellow human being. Religion becomes a matter of every moment, not just an hour of formal obligation each week. If I develop a sensitivity for each human being, I listen to God's voice in their speech, and feel the touch of the Spirit when they touch or reach out to me. Jesus meditated and prayed by becoming aware of the Spirit/Breath within his own breathing. Is this not a very natural and easy form of prayer? The challenge is to breathe in the Spirit of the people I meet each day and come to love.

This personalized religion leads to the possibility of an amazing source of vitality and strength that has been called the "Communion of Saints." Essentially it means that we do not travel alone through life. Fellow companions are deceased loved ones whom I call on in the Spirit, be they deceased spouse, parent, or friend, and trust they will be present to me. This same energy is present in regard to the living. Even if they are thousands of miles away, I experience their loving presence and help at any moment through the connecting web of the Spirit-Fire uniting us at the depths of our being.

It is this inter-connection and interrelationship that lies at the heart of the importance of both Mary Magdalene and Mary, his mother, to Jesus. They were not simply bystanders or observers of the great moments of his life, especially the cross. They were participators and co-actors with him at the deepest levels of existence and Spirit. We are indebted to them for bringing out the greatest insights of Jesus' message as addressed to the personal world of women and children. As such the two Marys are not just figures from the past. They are eternally associated with Jesus and forever play an essential role in bringing out the feminine face of God.

15. In Celebration of Women

Carolyn Grassi

Annunciation

Is the Annunciation to Mary the most painted theme of woman?
. . . inexhaustible, each time painted or told, another denoue-
ment is disclosed. And isn't it appropriate that she is completely
clothes, as if she knew we were privy to this most intimate
moment for a woman, she is about to conceive. We are watching,
waiting fro her response, as the angel approaches, as God
through the open window sends his Spirit Dove with flamed
throat to her earth, as she sits with book on her lap, placing
it to the side on the table, bowing her head slightly, as if fully
aware of what is happening, what consequences will follow,
what an honor's occurring — that God needs to enter her body,
to be formed as her child. So familiar the promise from the
Jewish Scriptures, reading them when the angel appears, so
her concent is emotional, intellectual, political; she's given it a
great deal of thought, her "yes" springs from her breast, the
vividness in her capacity to contain everything asked — to bear,
absorb, transform life, both the beauty and form of the Word

145

and its content. No wonder her response is without pride, she inclines her head in joy; the privilege felt in every muscle and fiber of her being. Her heart is on fire in song, after the simple and moving: "I am ready . . . come." The breaking out of: "My soul magnifies God. . . ."

Annunciation

newly formed grace
white feathered dove with scarlet throat
diving down to her breast
his breath opening folds of fire

the purple cloth parted
the pearl of great price freed
the winged messenger kisses her hand
the unexpected whispered secret

on her tongue-tip a song
climates change poles magnetize
nations settle in peace
lovers forge fidelity

God's partner
dancing with yes
Paradise as possible
beginning in her womb

Annunciation

this room's revelation
painted hundreds of times in man's imagination
a curtained space felt by countless women
readied by meditation her vivacious life
the seed spinning as a star touching her earth
a great love adhering to her womb
shaping details for the first time
her eyes color subtle hands rhythmed walk

his secret growing visible in her body
she can't hide it even if she wanted
feelings concentrated on forming the finest fruit
words the world's wanted rushing in her breast
every "yes" a line of blue through translucent skin
perfecting a tiny form ancient soul of the universe
strong arms thick reflective hair tender songs
maturing in her center this child of hers

Virgin and Child

as the dove's desired home
   God's tender intimacy
relaxed arms embracing the universe
   creation's hands miniaturize at her breast
she inclines a listening ear
   breath beside breath as air to earth's surfaces
rising sun dazzling center her sweetness

At the Agnus Dei

as a young bride welcomed
a new home language family
crowned as queen
never seeing your mother again

devoting yourself to a new people
marrying their hopes
from your body's generosity
creating their future

your girl's laughter turning
in graceful reserve
necessary finally
as a protective privacy

your Son as a lamb led to slaughter
piercing your heart with seven swords
gathering forgiveness in your breast
sweet golden fleece our holy grail

Resurrection

your pleasure   God's son   departs through childhood's door
reluctant leave-taking   in the desert   a myrtle flower's caress
he longs to touch the white furred dove
he drinks honey   sheltering his eyes at noon
under the palm tree cicadas laugh   are restless
caravans cross sanded moonlight for home

on the cave's shelf his white wrapping creased in four
your palm print   grief folded inside   between your breasts
memory's blood   milk   giving breath in pitch black December
now   a similar standing near rowed daffodils   calling his
name
the olive tree quivers against his weight   nests sway against
the sky
morning breaks the answer in two   who gives light to whom

Magdalene's Coronation (The Magdalene Church, Paris)

she rises over the high altar   surrounded by angels
their arms reach round her legs with incense songs

this woman who depended on man's regard
who knew labels of scorn as society's outcast

she shaded beauty in private corners
yellow   perfuming   lavender

a brief a life as the violet
knowing her gifts fading fast

she chose love over duty
beauty and tenderness as primary

she endures in the senses' memory
a resplendant advocate for the earthy

she wears a white rose in her black hair
pearls over her heart   pleasure as an art

she's mistress of her fate   surrendering
remembrance   as his beloved friend

she is without a child at her breast
praying at the back of the church

believing as women before and after
sons and daughters will someday come

Mary Magdalene, A Possibility

no proofs exist   no letters saved in bureaus
no photos left   no diaries in black ink

only imagination's capacity
what compassion wishes   believes

let us say she was brilliant
(meaning Sartre's definition:

sensibility and intelligence in the eyes)
standing out in a crowd

she was unaffected   resisting the expected
knowing when his gaze turned to her

releasing her tears   touching his skin
perfuming his feet with her thick hair

how he knew her voice   ideas   desires
necessary for his existence   a womanly essence

she was moved by fragile things   as a child   a rose
guarding their strengths   transposing resilience

she named details with grace
a collaboration   an anonymous love

lasting in legend as with Juliet   Heloise   Isolde
how time concentrates in brevity all its loveliness

Apocalypse

if you want me
I'm underground in labyrinths wells crypts
I rise like the lotus from murky waters
crimson petals in a blue green sky
over the plain at Chartres a jewel set on the city's hill

through my portal a welcoming song
at my tableside make yourself at home
visit me at altars near blond candles vased flowers
find my hands as vessels of understanding
believing everything's possible

know my contours shape forgotten names
Blanche Anne Eleanor Irene Antonia Florence Therese
I suggest everywoman's beauty
clothed with twelve stars
a crescent moon a snake under my feet*

*The Apocalypse

Notre Dame

you dream his future as you hold him in your arms
without thought of personal ambitions
not realizing his beauty features your face
his charm   intelligent   your grace made man

is this why you're so approachable
empty of self   radiantly close
your hand illustrates understanding
exposing in every line   how you love

now I wander your ancient residences   Chartres   Reims
Paris
struck by glances   once given   that continually give
a Queen ruling the twin domains of heaven and earth
carrying in your left arm   on your hip   the infant God

I find you sitting in the garden pavilion   overlooking the lake
holding him on your lap and in your right hand an Anjou pear
as he counts berries on a string   pages in the Book of Hours
blow back
sparrows sway on a rose bush   red-orange on white

I want to kiss the earth where you walked
how men and women used to for their king
pressing lips to where you stood on the grass
letting your fragrance pierce me as the white dove

Mary Magdalene in the Garden

(after a painting by Peter Paul Rubens)

the lilies have broken the ground
the scarlet tulips against the dark earth
in the distance two figures by the cave
they cannot see what she is doing

a woman kneeling beside a man
reaching in a graceful gesture
as all women who love
when instinct's developed in the body

and he understands her   knowing in himself
the same need rising   but conscious
of having to leave   wanting to spare her
his words burn   "do not touch me"

and whoever is watching   wanting to cast a stone
would only bring it back into their own hearts
not remembering how the promise was kept
God knew fully the feeling of flesh and blood

I think of her over the high altar
in her church "The Madeleine" in Paris
with four strong angels surrounding her legs
lifting her ecstasy   at last   into its sweet reward

and the powerful intention   a graceful burning
songs on the organ curve round her
and nothing   not even the angels' circle   holds her back
she is ready   rising to meet him who waits for her return

At the Virgin's Death

she closed her eyes   the man nearest stopped still

placing his hand over her heart   no pulse was felt

she departed as most women   without a trace

except in the features of her children   that is why

tears form at the corner of the poet's eyes

he is unsure of his capacity to recall her

he has no magical verse up his sleeve   he's an unknown

how will he find words for her to live as if her skin's warm

he's memorizing its texture   the curve of her lips
   her intelligent brows

the fragrance of her blue shawl   unforgettable
   as after dinner

he dreams her standing in the doorway of the small house
   facing seaward

the wind before her   the urgency to go   Paris lighting the
   violet sky

her tempered words   offered as homemade bread   warm
   hearty   sweet

her enormous strength when at a task   lifting bales of wheat

carrying the child in her belly under the hot grape arbor

same as the steady giving herself   day in and day out

sacrificing her dreams for a time or forever

she leaves as women before   effaced for a century or longer

yet   in this carving on the facade of Chartres

the poet's stunned by the expression in her sleeping face

not that he is a prince come to kiss her awake

not that he could teach her anything she did not already know

not that he will assume a position of advisor   mentor

not that she asks him to be generous   the time's past for that

no   her sort of truth behind the veiled lids   startles in their
wisdom

for the first time in his life   a woman makes him speechless

he enters her church   waiting for her to emerge in his silence